Hidden Meanings:
A Study of the Founding Symbols of Civilization

Hidden Meanings:
A Study of the Founding Symbols of Civilization

Laird Scranton

For Ogotemmeli,
Marcel Griaule & Germaine Dieterlen

Acknowledgments

This book would not have been possible without the support and help of friends and family. In particular, I would like to thank my wife Risa, son Isaac and daughter Hannah for their support and forebearance. I am also very grateful for the generous support, encouragement and friendship of Teresa Vergani, whose insights into Dogon symbols have been a great help. I would like to thank Time, Inc. and Eliot Elisofon for the use of his stunning photograph as the cover of this book. I am also indebted to Doug Kenyon at Atlantis Rising Magazine for printing a related article of mine on Dogon symbols, and to Martin Gray for the use of his beautiful photograph to illustrate that same article. I have greatly appreciated the enthusiasm and support of Ida Moffett Harrison and Stephen C. Infantino, whose careful work on *The Pale Fox* has proved so pivotal to my effort, and am indebted to Mr. Nataki at Afrikan World Books in Baltimore for generously allowing me to quote from that work. I would also like to thank the many friends and family members who have allowed me to use them as sounding boards for my ideas (sometimes against their will), including Lynda Falkenstein, Sue and Howard Sherer, Will Newman and Sue Clark, David and Kathy Scranton, Cathy Agnello Brown, Madeleine Bohrer, John Gardenier, Bill Churchman, Eric Infante, Dave Zimmer, Doris Schwaller, all of the ladies at Monroe Pediatrics, Desiree and Andre Krueger, Bill Przylucki, Jason Colavito, Michael Sherer, Raffi Arenos, and my mother Peg Scranton for proofreading and commenting on early drafts of my manuscript. And last but not least, to cousin Harvey Kornit–many psychic thanks for the copy of *Ancient Near Eastern Texts*.

Contents

Chapter 1: Introduction

From the first days of human civilization and from the very dawn of history, the ideas of myth and religion have been expressed in symbols. Even in the earliest times, these symbols took many different forms, starting out as simple drawings and figures, and evolving over time into sophisticated pictograms, hieroglyphs, icons and idols. No doubt there was a direct connection at first between each symbol and its meaning–as simple and direct as the painting of a bison on a cave wall. After all, a pictogram–the simplest form of a word–is just a drawing that depicts an object or an idea, and a drawing would be the most obvious choice as a symbol to represent an object. Even when we look at simple hieroglyphs, it is often possible to get a direct sense of meaning simply from the figures that represent it–as in the case of the Egyptian hieroglyph for water, which is represented by three wavy, waterlike lines. But as early societies became more complex and their concepts grew more sophisticated, symbols tended to become more abstract and obscure, so as time passed, the relationship between symbol and meaning became clouded.

Many of the mythological gods of ancient societies started out as the personification of a fundamental idea, religious concept, force of nature, or aspect of human nature–like *Poseidon*, the Greek god of the sea, or *Venus*, the Roman goddess of love. Some were worshipped as agricultural gods, immortal beings whose job it was to oversee the cycles of the growing season, like the Greek god of wine, *Dionysus*. Others, like the Roman god *Jupiter*, were seen as humanlike counterparts of planets or stars, whose actions in myth may have reflected actual movements of heavenly bodies. Some gods came to be associated with specific animals and often took on the noble (or ignoble) attributes of those animals–in some cultures, even to the extent that their images were drawn as part animal and part human, like the Ibis-headed Egyptian god *Thoth*. Sometimes gods and symbols were assigned the value of a number, which gave them an order of rank, and lent special significance to them as part of a system of numerology.

It was common for early cultures to take great care in the placement and orientation of buildings and temples. Many of the most elaborate structures were painstakingly aligned to the cardinal points of north, south, east and west, or were designed to include key features, like a doorway or an arch, that pointed to some recurring astronomical or calendric event, like a solstice or an eclipse. Most of us have heard stories about the great pyramid of Mexico whose shadow, on an appointed day of the year, forms the image of a slithering serpent on the ground, or have read theories about Stonehenge and its possible astronomical uses. Some of the earliest civilizations assigned symbolic relationships between structures and the constellations or star-groups they faced, almost as a reminder to us of the great preoccupation of early societies with astronomy. In fact, some researchers cite examples of whole complexes of buildings that may have been conceived as massive representations of a single religious or astronomical concept, or as star-maps of the sky as it might have looked in some remote age. During early historic times, there seems to have been a global urgency among emerging cultures to create immense, monolithic structures like the statues of Easter Island or the great pyramids of Egypt. Such construction projects involved the efforts of whole communities over many years to produce lasting monuments in stone whose practical purposes, if any, are largely unknown to modern scholars.

In the ancient writings that have passed down to us on

papyrus scrolls, clay tablets, and stone carvings, it is rare to find a clear explanation of what these early symbols mean, so modern scholars can only infer their possible meanings from context, comparison, supposition, and other clues. Each interpretation is subject to the uncertainties of mistranslation between languages, and often relies on fragmentary sources that may have been displaced in time by hundreds or thousands of years from the original concept or symbol. Worse yet, some symbols seem to take on different attributes in different contexts, as if their meanings had evolved over a period of time or changed from region to region. Even within a single culture, rival cult-centers might place emphasis on different gods, favor one god over another, or combine a regional god with a local deity. In fact, it was not uncommon for a single god to be called by different names in neighboring locales, thus multiplying the apparent number of gods and greatly adding to the confusion of modern students and historians. All of these factors combine to leave a great deal of room for interpretation and discussion when trying to understand the specific use or meaning of any given symbol. In recent years, it is likely that there have been as many scholarly attempts to interpret these symbols as there have been researchers–and yet still for many symbols, the traditionally-accepted meanings fail to ring true.

As we become more familiar with the many gods, images and symbols, it is hard not to notice obvious similarities between symbols and stories of the very earliest civilizations and religions. This has caused some researchers like Sir Wallace Budge–the author of the Egyptian hieroglyphic dictionary–to wonder whether as a group they could have derived from some single common source. These similarities cross the boundaries of oceans and continents, transcend ethnic groups, and have been noticed, pondered and puzzled-over by researchers for generation after generation. But a sketchy archeological record leaves us with few clues as to what possible source that might have been, and presently there is not much believable evidence that can attest to the existence in more remote times of a culture that could have exerted this kind of global influence.

Ancient symbols have significance across many fields of academic study, and stand at the root of religion, astronomy, mathematics, archeology, art, philosophy, linguistics and medicine–in fact, virtually every traditional school of human study. This may be why, over the past two thousand years, there has been such unfailing interest in understanding and knowing about these compelling symbols. During the course of the past two centuries alone, the history of archeology is filled with stories of amateur and professional scholars so thoroughly fixated on ancient societies and their symbols that they abandoned successful professional and personal lives, traveled enormous distances, spent great fortunes, and endured harsh living conditions and inhospitable work environments–just to gain an understanding of the symbols. But even for those willing to endure and overcome all of the physical and financial obstacles, the ancient symbols themselves present a formidable puzzle–partly because of their sheer number, partly because of the complex symbolism that seems to be associated with them, and partly because of the great length of time that has passed since they were used and understood. It is no wonder, then, that so many of these efforts have met with such limited success, or that our progress in understanding these symbols has been so slow.

The purpose of this study is to learn more about these ancient symbols, not by way of trips to exotic lands, archeological digs or crawling through ancient dusty tombs, but by the comparison of symbols between cultures, an exercise that may tell us more about their origins, forms, uses and meanings. Through these comparisons, we hope to show whether the symbols could have come from a common source, identify which symbols might have originated with that source, and learn something more about what the symbols mean and how they relate to each other.

If we hope to make any sense of the tangle of gods and images that grew out of thousands of years of ancient history, it makes sense that we simplify the task by starting with the oldest and most basic set of symbols—a smaller, more manageable, and more significant group—one that can be compared more easily across cultures. We know that these symbols can be found and identified, because they are the ones that turn up again and again, from generation to generation and society to society. In order to segregate these symbols, and since often times no one can say how truly ancient any given symbol might be, I have identified the period of 3400 BC—the approximate date of the emergence of the Egyptian civilization and of writing in Sumer—as a reference point. In other words, for a symbol to belong in this group, there should be evidence that it dates from the earliest days of the Egyptian civilization. Of the possible cultures to be used as a basis for comparison, I have selected the ancient Egyptian civilization and the modern Dogon tribe of Mali, with reference as needed to others such as the Sumerian, Babylonian and Akkadian civilizations.

There are many reasons why the Dogon religion should be placed in the role of the standard against which the others are compared. First, it includes a rich set of elements shared commonly by other religions. Many of the Dogon religious symbols and stories can also be found in the Egyptian and Sumerian religions, and Dogon society shares many of its cultural traditions with the people of ancient Egypt. The similarities between Egyptian rituals and those of Ethiopian Africa were noted as far back as Herodotus, the ancient historian, and even he declined to speculate as to which might be the older. Likewise, the Dogon religion shares many of its rituals with Judaism, such as the wearing of skull caps and prayer shawls, the practice of circumcision, and the celebration of a Jubilee year. Perhaps most importantly, Dogon society represents a living modern culture—one that is able to provide understandable meanings for its rituals and symbols and express them in modern terms. While it is hard to believe that some aspects of the Dogon religion have not changed or evolved over time, Dogon society–much like that of the ancient Egyptians themselves–seems to have retained a remarkable degree of coherence and consistency. Much of the credit for this must be given to the way in which the daily acts of Dogon life reinforce the symbols of the Dogon religion. For all of these reasons, the Dogon religion provides an excellent starting point for the kind of comparative study we propose.

For the purposes of understanding the Dogon culture and religion, this study relies on the works of Marcel Griaule and Germaine Dieterlen, two French anthropologists who lived among the Dogon and studied their customs and rituals during the 1930's, 40's and 50's. Griaule and Dieterlen recorded their observations about the Dogon in four principal works to which there are references throughout this study. The first is a book entitled **Conversations With Ogotemmeli**, a journal of Marcel Griaule's 33-day introduction to the Dogon religion by a knowledgeable Dogon priest named Ogotemmeli. The second is a finished study of the Dogon religion written by Germaine Dieterlen after the death of Marcel Griaule entitled **The Pale Fox**. The third is an article by Griaule and Dieterlen that discusses Dogon religious knowledge relating to the star system of Sirius, entitled **A Sudanese Sirius System**. The last is an article written by Marcel Griaule and Germaine Dieterlen entitled **The Dogon**, part of an anthology of articles by a variety of authors discussing the cosmologies of African tribes called **African Worlds**.

The authenticity of Dogon cosmology has been recently called into question by anthropologists such as Walter Van Beek, who studied the tribe in the 1980's and 90's. Van Beek finds no evidence of a native Dogon cosmology, and concludes that the Dogon priests simply invented one to satisfy the insistent questions of Marcel Griaule. However, this study will indentify many esoteric similarities between Dogon mythological and cosmological symbols and words and those of ancient Egypt which are consistent with other known Dogon/Egyptian cultural similarites. The extent and depth of these similarities all but preclude the possibility that what was presented by the Dogon priests as Dogon cosmology could have been the product of casual priestly invention.

Much of this study will focus on the creation stories of these various cultures, in an effort to identify similar and dissimilar aspects. If, in fact, these separate creation stories came from a single earlier source, then the elements they share in common are likely to have originated with that source. As we proceed, we have a variety of tools at our disposal to aid us in that effort. For one, we can compare individual symbols and how they were used by each culture. We can refer to ancient inscriptions and documents and what they tell us about the symbols. We can contrast various written and oral myths, and compare pertinent drawings of each culture. We can discuss similarities of religious rituals and cultural habits. We can test what we learn against the statements of later historians and the mythologies of later cultures. And perhaps most importantly, we can examine linguistic similarities–words that sound alike and have similar meanings, or equivalent concepts that are expressed in a similar way.

The Egyptian hieroglyphs provide us with a unique method for validating linguistic and conceptual similarities. One hallmark of the Egyptian hieroglyphs is that they remained remarkably unchanged in form from their first appearance around 3000 BC to their last use some 3000 years later. Although many new glyphs or characters were added during that period of time, the form and grammar of hieroglyphic writing remained so remarkably constant that an Egyptian scribe working in 700 BC would have been quite able to read and understand an inscription written 2000 years earlier. Moreover, hieroglyphic writing worked to establish meaning on two levels at the same time. The characters of the hieroglyph combined to form phonetic words much like the letters of an alphabet. But the pictures used to draw the hieroglyphic phrases often lent additional nuances of meaning to the words, much like the subtitles of a foreign movie. What this means is that, even if a given Egyptian word evolved in meaning over thousands of years, we might still find traces of an original meaning in the hieroglyphic characters that were used to express it. It should be noted here that, unless otherwise specifically stated, all references in this work to Egyptian hieroglyphs, their forms and meanings are taken from *An Egyptian Hieroglyphic Dictionary* by Sir E.A. Wallis Budge.

Chapter 2: Themes Of The Ancient Creation Stories

Creation stories are among the earliest religious artifacts of ancient societies. They presumably evolved first as oral traditions, only later to be put down in written form as emerging civilizations matured. In some cases like the Sumerian culture, no explicit written creation story has survived, however there are many references to the gods of creation and their attributes and actions in non-religious texts which make it possible to reconstruct the flow of an original narrative. The creation tradition of any single culture tended to evolve over time, often with variations from region to region, so scholars are sometimes left with more than one creation story or more than one version of the same story within a given society.

The oldest creation stories center around a surprisingly constant set of themes. If we look at these themes as they appear in the Dogon religion, we find that they can be grouped into two distinct storylines, which I call the *surface storyline* and the *deep storyline*. In some religions like the ancient Egyptian and modern Dogon religion, candidates for the priesthood were first introduced to a surface story that established a context for the various religious symbols and concepts, then graduated to a deeper story that further defined the inner teachings of the religion. The Dogon tell us that one purpose of this approach was to hold back or disguise the innermost secrets of the religion from all but the most committed of candidates.

For most societies, the surface storyline included some or all of the following elements. A self-created god emerges from the waters of chaos. The Dogon call this their one true god *Amma*; the corresponding Egyptian god is known as *Amen*, and an equivalent Sumerian goddess called *Nammu* bears the title of *Ama.Tu.An.Ki*. This self-formed god creates a series of godlike entities in pairs, usually eight in number. In the tradition of Heliopolis, these eight were *Shu and Tefnut, Geb and Nut, Isis and Osiris, and Seth and Nephthys*. The members of the four pairs are usually said to be *male and female*, or are cast as opposites–like *darkness and light* or *day and night*. The stars and planets, earth and moon are formed. Depending on the tradition, either the self-created god or one of the emergent gods creates the first man and woman, often from clay. In some cultures the eight paired entities take on the aspect of ancestors of man, like the eight ancestors of the Dogon and the eight Anunnaki of the Sumerians. Many times these same ancestors play the role of educators who teach the skills of civilization to mankind and sometimes serve as founding members of the original families of mankind, ultimately giving birth to eighty (or in some cultures, forty) offspring. The most revered or eldest of these ancestors may carry a name similar to *Leve, Lebe, or Levi*.

The deep storyline typically includes more intimate details about the creation of the formed universe from the unformed universe than the surface story. Typically, the unformed universe is described as an egg–the Dogon refer to it as *Amma's egg*–which contains all of the *seeds or signs of the world*. In some cultures these signs are represented as the letters of the alphabet, while in others they are simply identified as the seeds of the world to come. Specific details of the storyline vary from culture to culture– for example, in the creation tradition of Hermopolis in Egypt pairs of serpents and frogs create the egg. Commonly, an unspecified force causes this cosmic egg to open–the Dogon call it the *opening of Amma's eyes*–releasing a whirlwind that ultimately forms the spiraling galaxies of stars and planets.

Implied throughout these storylines are a basic set of principles which can be observed in the oldest myths of many cultures, and which the Dogon take great care to explicitly define. The first is the *principle of twinness*, which is apparent in Dogon mythology from the earliest moment of creation. For the Dogon, the universe actually consists of two creations, one of which we can see and one of which we cannot see. In the surface story of the Dogon, the initial act of the self-created god *Amma* is to form a perfect twin pair, which the Dogon call the *Nummo or Nommo*. Each of the creative acts that follow occur in pairs. This same pattern can be seen in the dominant Egyptian creation traditions of Heliopolis and Hermopolis, both of which describe an initial set of emergent godlike entities created in pairs.

A second guiding principle that applies to these sets of twins is the *pairing of male and female*. In some societies we see this principle first expressed in the form of a self-created god who is defined as being *both male and female*, or who is considered to be androgynous, followed by four male/female pairs of emergent gods and goddesses. Sometimes, this principle is alternately expressed as the *pairing of opposites*, like *order and chaos*, or in some cases in the form of *positive and negative* like *Yin and Yang*.

These two principles of twinness and the pairing of opposites are present in all aspects of Dogon culture. For example, the Dogon establish their villages and districts in pairs, which they refer to as *upper and lower*. We can see this same custom reflected in the traditional organization of ancient Egypt into two lands, one called *Upper Egypt* and the other called *Lower Egypt*. Similarly, the two Egyptian lands took "opposing" colors–red and white–as their standards, colors which for some modern African tribes represent *success in cattle herding* and *success in agriculture*, respectively. This implies a kind of deliberate division of labor in ancient Egypt that is not atypical of modern Dogon culture, wherein a given plot of land is divided between those who farm and others who forge the tools and implements of farming. The metalworkers receive a share of the crop raised on the plot, but are forbidden to raise crops themselves.

Beyond these basic guiding principles there are also symbols that are central to the Dogon creation narrative and which turn up again and again in the earliest creation stories. The first is the image of the *spiraling coil*, which expresses itself in many different forms and settings. We see it in images of the *ram's horns*, which are found in nature in two incarnations–*laterally spiraling* and *coiled*. We see it in the *serpent*, a creature which moves in a *laterally spiraling motion* and rests in a *coil*. The serpent symbol is perhaps the single most pervasive and persistent image of the oldest mythologies and cultures. We may also see the image of the spiraling coil in the many ancient references to *whirlwinds and storms*.

Equal in importance to the *spiraling coil* is the symbol of *water*. In the earliest mythologies, the original self-created god is usually said to emerge from the *primordial waters* or the *waters of chaos*. Many of the dominant gods and goddesses–like the Egyptian god *Atum* and the *Nummo* of the Dogon–are specifically said to represent water. In fact, in the Dogon language, the word *Nummo* means *water*. Likewise, the Sumerian god *Enki* is understood to symbolize the *waters of the earth*, while his counterpart *Enlil* is known to represent the *air as a kind of fluid* that fills the space between the earth and sky.

Another important symbol that is central to the oldest mythologies is that of *clay*, which also appears in many forms. In the Dogon creation story, the planets are like *pellets of clay* flung out into space at the opening of *Amma's egg*, and the sun is compared to a *pot of clay* which has been raised to a high heat. In many early mythologies, we are told that the first man and woman are *created from clay*—the trail of this same creational theme can be seen in the later Greek myth of Prometheus, who is said to have molded mankind from clay. Similar primal links to clay and water can be found in the Egyptian religion, as is the case with the Egyptian word *nun*, which was used to express the concept of the *primordial waters*. The hieroglyphic characters used to write the word *nun* consist of *three clay pots* and *three wavy lines of water*, which shows that the image of the clay pot may also have been an original part of Egyptian creation tradition:

The earliest creation stories place recurring emphasis on the numbers *two and eight*. For instance, the Dogon say that the *Nummo* was the perfect twin pair, and the sun is surrounded by a spiral of copper with eight turns. The original Ennead of Egypt consisted of eight gods, just as there were said to be eight original Sumerian Anunnaki.

Numerology is a frequent feature of the earliest religions, and there is a kind of uniformity in the assignment of numbers and meanings among many different cultures. For example, one hallmark of the most ancient religions is that the first ten numbers are represented by the first ten letters of the alphabet, and the number ten is considered to be the "perfect" number. The name for the letter representing ten is also often seen as a name for god. Even today we can see traces of this kind of pattern in the Spanish language, where the word Dios means *God* while the word Dies means *ten*. Another example of this can be found in the very name of *Judaism* itself, which is presumably taken from the tenth letter of the Hebrew alphabet, *yud*. For the Dogon, other specific numbers have special numerological significance;

three is the number of the male; *four* is the number of the female; *seven* is the number of the individual and of the *master of language*; *eight* is the number of *language itself*. *Nine* is the number of chieftainship. Echoes of this plan of numerology can be found in many other cultures of the world. For instance, in ancient Egyptian art and sculpture, the number *nine* can often be found on renderings of the Pharaoh, a custom that is perhaps another expression of the Dogon numerological symbol for chieftainship.

There are obvious similarities in the basic plotline and structure of the creation stories of the Dogon, the ancient Egyptians, and the ancient Sumerians. These similarities are reflected in the names, sequence, acts, and configuration of gods and goddesses said to emerge from the waters at the time of creation, and are made more obvious by the chart below:

DOGON	EGYPTIAN	SUMERIAN
Amma	Amen/Atum	Ama.Tu.An.Ki/Nammu
Male & female Nummo	Nehmmu/Khnoum	Enki & Enlil
8 ancestors	8 Ennead gods plus	8 Anunnakki
8 familes/80 members	Horus	40 Anunnakki

The many similarities between of the gods of Egypt and those of Mesopotamia have been noticed over the years by many observers, and some have sought to find underlying reasons for the similarities. Sir E.A. Wallis Budge, author of the hieroglyphic dictionary, addresses himself in **The Gods of the Egyptians** to the perplexing issue of these similarities.

> "It is surprising therefore to find so much similarity existing between the primeval gods of Sumer and those of Egypt, especially as the resemblance cannot be the result of borrowing. It is out of the question to assume that Ashur-banipal's editors borrowed the system from Egypt, or that the literary men of

the time of Seti I borrowed their ideas from the *lite-rati* of Babylonia or Assyria, and we are therefore driven to the conclusion that both the Sumerians and the early Egyptians derived their primeval gods from some common but exceedingly ancient source. The similarity between the two companies of gods seems to be too close to be accidental. " (*The Gods of the Egyptians* p. 290)

Likewise, respected members of the modern-day academic community are also quite aware of the types of correlations that exist between the ancient Egyptian religion and modern Dogon mythology. Nicholas Grimal comments on some of these similarities in his book *A History of Ancient Egypt*:

> "Anubis recalls the incestuous jackal in a Promethean role which existed prior to the Nummos among the Dogon people of Mali, whose cosmology also depends on eight original gods. There are further African links with Egypt: Amun, for instance, resembles the golden heavenly ram whose brow is adorned with horns and a gourd reminiscent of the solar disc; Osiris recalls Lebe, whose resurrection is announced by the regrowth of the millet; and finally, each individual was thought to be made up of a soul and a vital essence . . . which the Egyptians called the *ba* and the *ka*." (*A History of Ancient Egypt* p. 45)

In many of the earliest religions, the first three emergent gods and goddesses are said to represent–in one form or another–*water, air, and earth.* But the symbolism attached to these entities is usually somewhat complicated. Typically the goddess of the air is said to represent *humidity* or *the atmosphere,* or *air conceived as a fluid.* The god of the earth often represents in some complex way the *waters of the earth.* For reasons that have not been fully explained, there is a persistent intrusion of *water* into the symbolism of these earliest gods and goddesses that serves to complicate our understanding of their roles. The first self-created god or goddess in most cultures is typified by a kind of vagueness of description–often with few specific attributes or qualities assigned to him or her. Generally, the female member of the first twin pair of entities is associated with *air, the atmosphere, storms and the arts of weaving and language.* The male member is more often symbolized by a *ram, goat, or other horned animal and the arts of pottery and metalworking.* Thus in the Egyptian religion we have Khnoum, the ram-headed god associated with the Egyptian god *Ptah* and his potter's wheel and *Ptah* identified with the Greek god *Hephaistos,* the mythological blacksmith.

In and amongst these emergent gods and goddesses whose lineage is clearly stated comes another type of goddess whose relationship to the stories of creation is less clearly defined. Many of the earliest cultures honor an original *mother goddess,* often said to be the oldest of the gods and to have given birth to all of the other gods. The Dogon creation story makes no obvious reference to a separate goddess in this role, but the Sumerians assign this place to the goddess *Nammu,* whose title is *Ama.Tu.An.Ki.* In this title we can see possible roots of the names of the Dogon god *Amma* and the Sumerian god *Enki (An.Ki),* just as we see an obvious relationship between the Dogon word *Nummo* and the Sumerian name *Nammu.* Egyptian mythology also identifies an original mother goddess; one of the earliest Egyptian temples was founded by the first king of Egypt and dedicated to the goddess *Neith*–perhaps originally a Libyan goddess–who was said to be the mother of the numberless Egyptian gods.

Another concept of great importance to the earliest religions is the idea of the *cardinal points of the earth*–north, south, east and west. Many of the earliest religious symbols included features that were meant to represent the cardinal points, like the four corners of the Jewish *tallis*. It is a well known fact that important structures of the ancient world, like the Great Pyramid of Egypt, were carefully and deliberately aligned to the four cardinal points. In many early mythologies, the sky was said to be supported by four great posts or pillars, each of which was identified with one of the four cardinal points.

Another concept that is carefully defined by the Dogon religion and persistently found among other early religions is the concept of *the word*. The Dogon use this term literally to represent speech and language, but they also use it figuratively to mean the *acquisition of a skill or knowledge of a concept*. For example, in Dogon mythology the concept of clothing as exemplified by the first fiber skirt is said to represent the *first* Word, and mastery of the skill of *weaving* constitutes the *second* Word. In these examples, the concept of *the word* can be taken figuratively to mean instruction in civilizing skills–in essence, *words in the language of civilization*. A related concept of Dogon mythology is the notion of *words being woven into the cloth*. This concept is introduced with the statement that the vapor from the *Nummo's* breath as they spoke was absorbed into the strands of the first fiber skirt. Together these two Dogon concepts can be seen as the likely precursors of later Christian symbolism, which speaks often about the *word of God* and commonly refers to priests as *men of the cloth*.

Because these themes, symbols and concepts reappear so frequently in the earliest mythologies, their prominence makes them pivotal to any comparative understanding of those mythologies. Likewise, the Dogon creation tradition assumes an important role in this process of understanding because of its unique ability to explain these symbols and concepts in plain and understandable terms.

Chapter 3: The Dogon Creation Story

Before we can begin to make comparisons based on the symbols of the Dogon religion, we must first familiarize ourselves with the surface storyline of the Dogon creation story. Although the Dogon have a sophisticated spoken language and an extensive catalog of religious symbols and signs, they are not possessed of an actual written language, and so therefore there has been no indigenous written version of the Dogon creation story. Because of this, Marcel Griaule and Germaine Dieterlen found themselves faced with the formidable task of reconstructing a written story from various Dogon oral myths and drawings, and from the knowledge and insight of a group of elder Dogon priests. Dogon cosmology is actually shared by a small group of related tribes who live in close proximity to the Dogon, so the final written version came to include contributions from elders of each of the related tribes. Part of the challenge for the anthropologists was to reconcile differences between various versions of the myths in order to produce what amounts to a consensus of Dogon thought and belief. When appropriate, Griaule and Dieterlen included alternate versions of the same myth in their finished text, so as to accurately reflect differences in Dogon schools of thought. It is important to remember that, in the surface storyline, some of the original Dogon concepts were intentionally simplified and others made more complicated as a means of disguising references to the deepest secrets of the religion.

No doubt the surface narrative of the Dogon creation story is best expressed by Marcel Griaule's book *Conversations With Ogotemmeli*, a short work that reflects

Griaule's understanding of the Dogon religion based on several years of observation and thirty-three days of specific instruction by a Dogon priest. *The Pale Fox* represents a finished anthropological report on the Dogon religion, and includes a more detailed discussion of Dogon symbols and concepts, taken from what I call the deep storyline. Since our study, like many others, draws primarily from the works of Griaule and Dieterlen for information about the Dogon, any summary presented here of the surface creation story of the Dogon must necessarily be in paraphrase of Marcel Griaule's work in **Conversations With Ogotemmeli**.

The Dogon believe that the stars were created as pellets of earth flung out into space by the one true God, Amma. The sun and the moon were created by a process much like pottery, which was the first known invention of God. The sun is like a pot that has been fired until it is white-hot, then surrounded by a spiral of copper with eight turns. To create the earth, Amma squeezed a lump of clay in his hand and threw it away from himself in the same manner as the stars. The clay spread to the north and to the south (the top and the bottom) in a movement that was horizontal. By nature, the earth is female–looking at it flat, and considering the cardinal points of the compass as her appendages, it is like a woman lying on her back with her arms and legs spread. The anthill is her female organ. In the course of time, Amma tried to fertilize her, but in what was to be a breach of order in the universe, proper intercourse could not take place. In the universe, there is a principle of twin births, but this flawed union between God and earth created only one being, the jackal, which became the symbol of disorder and the difficulties of God. Later, having overcome the difficulty, God had intercourse with the earth again, this time successfully. Water, which is the divine seed, entered the womb of the earth and resulted in the birth of twins. Two beings were formed, which God created like water. They were green in color, and were half-human, half serpent. Their bodies were green and sleek all over and shiny like the surface of the water. These spirits were called Nummo and they were born perfect. They had eight members, and their number was eight, which is also the symbol of speech. They were of divine essence, which is the life-force of the world, and is water. The name Nummo is synonymous in the Dogon language with the word for water; to the Dogon, Nummo is water and the Nummo pair is present in all water–whether it be drinking water, water of the river, or water of storms. Griaule quotes Ogotemmeli as saying:

> 'The life-force of the earth is water. God moulded the earth with water. Blood too he made out of water. Even in a stone there is this force, for there is moisture in everything. But if Nummo is water, it also produces copper. When the sky is overcast, the sun's rays may be seen materializing on the misty horizon. These rays, excreted by the spirits, are of copper and are light. They are water too, because they uphold the earth's moisture as it rises. The Pair excrete light, because they are also light.' (Conversations With Ogotemmeli p. 19)

After the defilement of the earth during the first ill-fated attempt at intercourse, God decided to create man directly. He formed a womb and a male organ from two lumps of clay. These lumps developed into the first pair of humans, male and female. Man, who is usually born one at a time, violated the principle of twin births, so to atone for this, man was given two souls, one male and one female.

The first man and woman had intercourse with each other and gave birth in pairs to a series of eight children, who became the eight ancestors of the Dogon. The first four were male, the next four female. Griaule writes that, " . . . by a special dispensation, permitted only to them, they were able to fertilize themselves   ." In the beginning the eight ancestors did not know death, but lived on indefinitely.

The Nummo twins represent the ideal unit. When the Nummo looked down at the earth and saw it unclothed and speechless, they decided to put an end to the disorder and confusion. The Nummo came down to earth, bringing with them the fibers of plants created in heaven. From these fibers they created the first garment, which was made of two strands of ten fibers—one worn in front, the other in back. The way the fibers hung in spiraling coils was symbolic of the water of tornadoes and hurricanes, the fibers themselves were reminiscent of the sun, which dries up moisture, and were also like the speech of the Nummo which comes out in a warm vapor of water, the sound of which tapers off in spiraling coils. In this sense, the moisture of the words of the Nummo were transferred to the fibers of the garment. The Dogon call the creation of this fiber skirt the First Word.

In the anthill, the male Nummo assumed the role of the masculine element, and the female Nummo took the role of the female element. After a time, instinct led the oldest of the eight ancestors toward the anthill, wearing a wooden bowl on his head to protect him from rain. He put his feet into the opening of the anthill and sank in, all except the bowl, which became caught on the edges of the opening. This freed him from his role as a physical being and he was taken under the guidance of the Nummo pair. He followed the male Nummo into the depths of the earth, where, in the waters of the earth's womb, he curled up like a fetus and shrank to germinal form, and acquired the quality of water, the seed of God, and the essence of the two Nummo spirits. Just as the eight copper spirals give the sun its movement, the spiral of the Word gave the womb its regenerative movement. *All eight ancestors, one by one, had to be transformed in this way.*

To the Dogon, three is the number of the male element. Four is the number of the female element. The seventh in a series represents perfection, even though it is not inherently better than any of the others, because it is the sum of the male and female elements.

The words that the female Nummo spoke to herself turned into a spiral and entered into her sexual part, and the male Nummo helped her. These words are what the seventh ancestor learned while inside the womb. The seventh ancestor received perfect knowledge of the Second Word, which was not reserved for particular recipients, but was meant for all mankind. During this transformation, the seventh ancestor developed slowly in the womb of the earth. On the day when his transformation was complete, he emerged at sunrise and, using his teeth as weaver's reeds and the movement of his jaws to create a shuttle action, invented the art of weaving. While weaving, he imparted technical instruction so that people could understand the process, demonstrating by example the need for harmony between spiritual forces and physical actions. The words that the spirit spoke were woven into the cloth as it was created–they were the cloth, which was the Word. The Dogon call woven material soy, which means, "It is the spoken word". Soy also means seven, after the seventh ancestor.

The Nummo, acting on behalf of Amma, planned to initiate projects to improve and redeem mankind, but were concerned about the effect of contact between themselves, spiritual beings, and people of flesh and blood. So after the transformation of the eight ancestors, they were taken to heaven with the Nummo to learn the skills of civilization. Later, each was given one of the eight grains of heaven and they returned to live with men again, bringing with them their newly-learned skills.

Up until the time of the ancestors, people had lived in

holes dug in the soil. Now they noticed the shape of the anthill, which they found to be much better than their earthen holes. They copied its shape and made mud huts, added rooms and passageways, and began to use them to store food. This improved anthill was the precursor of the Granary, which would be introduced as the next divine concept, and which constituted the Third Word. The first Granary was shaped like a woven basket turned upside-down. It was round at the bottom, square and flat at the top, and wider at the bottom than the top. There were stairways with ten steps up the middle of each of the four sides, which faced toward the cardinal points of north, south, east and west. The door of the Granary was at the sixth step of the north side. Inside were two levels containing eight chambers. The structural features of the Granary had symbolic meaning:

The round base represented the sun. The square roof represented the sky. A circle in the center of the roof represented the moon.

The rise of each step was male, the tread was female. The combined total of forty steps (80 males and females) represented the eighty offspring of the eight ancestors.

Each stairway was associated with a constellation and a group of creatures. The north was associated with the Pleiades and represented men and fish. The south was associated with the belt of Orion and represented domesticated animals. The east was associated with Venus and represented birds, and the west was associated with what the Dogon called the long-tailed star, and represented wild animals, vegetables, and insects. The ten steps up each side of the granary represented different family orders of the animal and plant kingdoms.

When the first ancestor came down from heaven, he was standing on a square piece of heaven shaped like the Granary.

To the Dogon, there is also symbolism associated with the eight compartments of the Granary, four of which are on the lower level, and four on the upper. The compartments were separated by two intersecting partitions. The point at which these partitions met created a cup-shaped depression in the earth large enough to hold a round jar. The jar, which held grain or objects of value, was the center of the whole building. The compartments were numbered from 1 to 8, moving counter-clockwise around the lower level from the front/right compartment, then continuing on the upper level, starting with the front/right compartment. The Granary, like the earth in earlier descriptions, represented a woman lying on her back with her arms and legs spread—the jar was her womb, the four uprights which ended in the corners of the roof were her arms and legs. Her legs were on the north side, and the door represented her sexual parts. The woman also represented the sun, and her arms and legs, which supported the roof, represented the sky.

In another way, the Granary also represented the internal organs of the body, and showed the circulation of nourishment within a body. Nourishment flowed from the first two compartments, which represented the stomach and gizzard, then moved symbolically into the intestines (compartment 6) and then into all of the other compartments as symbolic blood and breath. From there it moved into the final compartments, which represented the liver and gall bladder. The Dogon consider breath to be vapor, a form of water, which is the sustaining principle of life.

Assembled on the flat roof of the Granary were the tools of a forge, which were to be used by the first ancestor to teach man to make iron tools for cultivating the land. The bellows were made out of two twin clay pots connected by a sheepskin. The shape of the two pots represent the sun.

The sheepskin is a symbol of the celestial Ram, which is the avatar, or animal representation, of the male Nummo. The hammer was an iron block with a handle shaped like a cone. The anvil was fixed in a beam of wood. The smith/ancestor had an iron bow and spindles for arrows. He shot one arrow into the center of the circle on the roof of the Granary, which represented the moon, and he wrapped a long thread around the shank to form a bobbin. He shot a second arrow into the air, which attached to the vault of the sky. Together with the Granary, this created an entire system of symbols:

> The Granary represented the new world-system. It defined a unit of volume. The height of each step was a unit of length, the cubit. A unit of area was provided by the flat roof, which was eight cubits by eight cubits. The square roof and the round base were examples of the two primary geometric figures. Symbolically, the Granary represented the shape of iron. It was also the head of the hammer, which is male, and represented the four-sided anvil, which is female. Additionally, it was the webbed-hand of the Nummo, of which the hammer was also an image. Finally, it represented the female body, which is the female element of the smith, who like all beings, was dual in nature.

To create the original fire of the smithy, the ancestor stole embers, which were a piece of the sun, from the workshop of the Nummo, who are heaven's smiths. To steal the embers, he used a 'robber's stick' the crook of which opened in a slit that was like an open mouth. On the way back to the granary/smithy, the ancestor accidentally dropped some embers and had to come back to pick them up. He then fled toward the Granary, but in the anxiety of his escape, could not locate its entrance. He went around it several times before he found the steps and climbed up to the flat roof, where he hid the embers in one of the skins of the bellows. He exclaimed "Gouya!", which means "Stolen!". Today in the Dogon language, gouya means "granary". It is a reminder that there would be no grain to store without the fire of the smithy, from which iron hoes are made.

The art of pottery came to be associated with the smithy. The story is that the wife of the smithy had made a pot, shaped like the clay pots of the bellows, which she was letting dry in the sun. Hoping it would dry more quickly, she moved it closer to the fire of the smithy and found that the heat made the pot harden. From that day on, she came to be in the habit of firing her pots. Pottery was originally the exclusive domain of the wives of the smithies, but later it became permissible for any woman to practice pottery.

At this point, the ancestor was ready to begin the work of civilization, starting with the teaching of agriculture. He came down the north stairway and measured out a square field, eighty cubits on each side, oriented to the cardinal points of north, south, east and west, just like the Granary. The field was divided into eight-by-eighty units, each 1-cubit square, which were distributed among the families of the eight ancestors. Mud houses for the families were built along the center line of the land, which ran from north to south. The smithy was established to the north of this line. The Dogon believed that the earth had been pure when it was originally created, but the incident of the birth of the Jackal made it impure and had disrupted the world order. Agriculture was a symbol for the restoration of order to the pure earth, and wherever agriculture and civilization spread, the impurity of the earth receded.

According to Ogotemmeli, the original method of cultivation was like weaving; it began on the north side and move from east to west, then back again. On each line, eight feet were planted, and the square consisted of eight lines, in memory of the eight ancestors and the eight seeds. The Dogon say that when a man clears new ground, makes a plot and builds a hut on the plot, his work is like weaving a cloth. In this way, the skill of agriculture is a form of weaving.

Although all eight families were of equal rank, the eighth had a special privilege. Seven is the number of the master of speech, whose job it was to teach speech, but eight is the number of speech itself. Because the oldest living Dogon man belonged to the eighth family, he of all living beings most truly represented the Word. His name was Lebe.

When the first ancestor, who was the smith, had finished his instruction, the seven other ancestors descended to teach their skills of civilization to man. These skills included leatherworking, music, and so on, and were taught in order of rank. But the eighth ancestor took his place out of turn, and came down before the seventh, who was the master of speech. This made the seventh ancestor so very angry that he turned against the others, took the form of a great serpent, and tried to remove the heavenly grains from the granary. The smith saw the serpent as an adversary, and in order to rid himself of it, advised men to kill the snake. Ogotemmeli considered this dispute a turning-point in the history of the world.

Chapter 4: Dogon Symbols and Meanings

The surface narrative of the Dogon creation story presents themes and incidents that should seem quite familiar to students of ancient mythologies. The sequence and manner in which the dominant godlike entities of the Dogon religion emerge is comparable to that of the earliest Egyptian, Sumerian and Akkadian religious traditions. The creation story narrative itself includes subplots that we find repeated in the later fables of Greek mythology, such as the incident in which the Dogon ancestor steals the fire of the Nummo. Likewise there are many obvious resemblances between Dogon symbolism and that of Mayan mythology—for example, both cultures conceive of the earth as a woman lying on her back, her arms and legs conceived as the cardinal points. The roughly pyramidal shape and dimensions of the Dogon granary call to mind the early mastabas of ancient Egypt, and we find many of the symbolic aspects of the Dogon granary repeated in the flat-topped pyramids of the Americas. The more familiar we become with the deep symbolism of the Dogon creation story, the more we will see that these similarities extend to some of the most remote corners of the world, and resonate with the mythologies of societies as diverse as the Maiori of New Zealand, the earliest cultures of Asia, and even the native tribes of North America.

If it is our goal to understand more about the meaning of Dogon religious symbols, then the most obvious place to start is with observations of the anthropologists who most closely studied them. Although Griaule and Dieterlen did not venture to interpret possible meanings of individual Dogon symbols beyond what the Dogon themselves state, it was their opinion that the Dogon religious system should be seen as much more than a simple tribal mythology. In their view, it represented a serious and careful discussion of the fundamental forces at work in the physical world. This opinion is openly and unambiguously stated in the various writings of Griaule and Dieterlen:

> "Having observed and studied everything within range of their perception, they have constructed an indigenous explanation of the manifestations of nature (anthropology, botany, zoology, geology, astronomy, anatomy, and physiology) as well as social facts (social structures, religious and political structures, crafts, arts, economy, etc.). The Dogon possess a system of signs or ideographs including several thousands, an astronomy and calendars, a numerical system, extensive physiological and anatomical knowledge, genetics, and a systematic pharmacopoeia . . . The world is conceived as a whole, this whole having been thought, realized, and organized by one creator God in a complete system which includes disorder . . . The development of Dogon thought, and hence the elaboration of concepts, proceeds by analogy and has constant recourse to the symbol . . . Thus, the symbol plays the role "of conveyor of knowledge . . . ." The value and efficacy of the symbol are such in this system, that the Dogon declare that it is not the thing itself, but "the symbol alone which is essential" . . . In the religious domain, this system is linked together by the existence of elaborate myths dealing with the fundamental notion of God, the history of the creation of the world, of the establishment of order and the appearance of disorder . . . The myth [which the Dogon call] *so tanie* 'astonishing word' which the Dogon consider to be 'real' history . . . constitutes here the whole of co-

herent themes of creation; this is why, by virtue of their coherence and their order of succession, they make up a "history of the universe," *aduno so tanie.* " (*The Pale Fox p.* 57-60)

"By no means . . . should the word of the myth be understood in its ordinary sense, as a childlike or fantastic, somewhat absurd poetic form. The myth is . . . only a means by which to explain something; it is a consciously composed lore of master ideas which may not be placed within reach of just anyone at any time . . . It conceals clear statements and coherent systems reserved for initiates, who alone have access to the 'deep knowledge'. The myths present themselves in layers, like the shells of a seed, and of their reasons for being is precisely to cover and conceal from the profane a precious seed which appears to belong rightly to a universal, valid body of knowledge." (*The PaleFox* p. 61)

"The Dogon myth does not relate facts merely involving adventures, rivalries between the gods, or the effects of love and hate . . . such as they are presented by other religions . . . Rather it shows evidence of serious examination of the very conditions of life and death; hence, its precise biological aspect . . . The myth presents a construction of the universe— from that of the stellar system down to that of the smallest grain . . . ." (*The Pale Fox* p. 70)

"Among the Dogon exoteric myths correspond to a 'superficial knowledge' common to the greater part of the population; on the other hand, esoteric myths, parallel to these, present other identifications and much wider connexions. Finally, within and beyond this totality of beliefs appears a logical scheme of symbols expressing a system of thought which cannot be described simply as myth. For this conceptual structure, when studied, reveals an internal coher-

ence, a secret wisdom, and an apprehension of ultimate realities equal to that which we Europeans conceive ourselves to have attained." (*African Worlds*
p.83)

Another useful reference when it comes to understanding Dogon words and phrases is the **Dictionaire Dogon**,
compiled by Genevieve Calame-Griaule, daughter of Marcel
Griaule and a respected anthropologist in her own right.
The dictionary confirms Marcel Griaule's translation of *aduno*
as "universe" and *so tanie* as "astonishing word". But a
close examination shows that the word *aduno* can also mean
"symbols", the word *so* can mean "to speak", and the
word *ta* means "to do something discreetly, or in a way that
does not transgress". So an alternate meaning for the phrase
aduno so tanie might well be "symbols that are spoken
about discreetly". A loose but more concise translation might
be "secret symbols" or "hidden symbols".

These statements by Griaule, Dieterlen and Calame-
Griaule lend strong encouragement to those who would seek
concrete meaning in the symbols of Dogon mythology. There
is no doubt that any search for serious meaning in the surface narrative of the creation story should focus first on
major themes of the myths, because it is to these ideas and
concepts that the storyline repeatedly draws our attention.
Among these themes, the first that comes to mind is that of
water, since previous discussion has shown water to be *the*
central image in each ancient mythology. It might seem
more than coincidental that every member of each triad of
gods is defined first in terms of water, most of the Dogon
and Egyptian symbols relating to creation refer back to water, and many of the Egyptian hieroglyphs pertaining to the
concepts of creation are expressed using the symbols of
water. So an obvious first step in an effort to assign meanings to the symbols would be to reconsider what we know
about water, starting with Marcel Griaule's statement of

Ogotemmeli's understanding of water. He quotes Ogotemmeli as saying:

> "The life-force of the earth is water. God moulded the earth with water. Blood too he made out of water. Even in a stone there is this force, for there is moisture in everything . . . When the sky is overcast, the sun's rays may be seen materializing on the misty horizon. These rays . . . are water, too, because they uphold the earth's moisture as it rises." (*Conversations With Ogotemmeli* p.19)

The Dogon understanding of nature of *water* as expressed by Ogotemmeli corresponds remarkably well with descriptions of water as they appear in a typical article from any given encyclopedia or reference book. Such articles reaffirm that living matter is primarily composed of water, that the major component of life-giving fluids in plants and animals is water, that water settles in rock beds beneath the earth and within rocks themselves, and that water vapor rises due to the heat of the sun, only to fall back to earth again as precipitation. The content of Ogotemmeli's description and that from any modern-day reference book, taken side by side, are strikingly and thoroughly similar–so completely so that the Dogon rendition could almost be inserted in place of the corresponding sentences of a typical article and not significantly alter the meaning. In fact, a student could learn nearly as much from Ogotemmeli's statements about water as from a modern encyclopedia. This fact lends support to Griaule and Dieterlen's assessment of the Dogon creation story as a serious presentation of fact, and provides us with a possible clue about the kind of information to be looked for in the myths. It suggests that what lies behind the symbols of the story is a kind of basic encyclopedic information–general, factual, true knowledge, organized and presented as if to inform.

A random survey of encyclopedia articles about water shows that most are organized in a similar and predictable way. First they present information about the molecular structure of water (H_2O), then tell about the three physical states of water (liquid, solid and vapor), then discuss the natural water cycle, explaining how water is evaporated to form clouds, which then cause precipitation, which falls to earth and collects in streams, rivers and groundwater, and eventually makes its way back to the sea to be evaporated in the form of clouds again. If Ogotemmeli's statements about water and those from our encyclopedia article are just coincidentally similar, then we would not expect the creation myths to include useful information about the molecular structure or physical states of water, nor would we expect to find discussion about the natural water cycle.

But when we re-examine the Dogon creation myth from this perspective and look specifically for information about water, what we find is somewhat surprising. The numbers *two and eight* are the numbers of the electron structure of water. Hydrogen provides the first two electrons as a twin pair of atoms, and oxygen supplies the additional eight electrons. If we suppose for a moment based on this fact that the perfect Nummo pair represent hydrogen, then what the Dogon say is quite true, that the Nummo pair is found in all water, whether it be water we drink, water of a river, or the water of storms. This information should not surprise us since the Dogon tell us again and again in the most explicit ways that Nummo is water. Likewise, the rays of the sun could be reasonably seen as the excrement of the Nummo since we know that solar energy is a by-product of the fusion of hydrogen atoms, which are in this sense of meaning the Nummo pair. So by simply assuming what the story plainly tells us to be true, that Nummo means water, we are able to explain what Marcel Griaule was not able to ascertain from Ogotemmeli's explanation, how a symbol that represents water could also represent "the burning rays of the sun."

The Dogon also express their enigmatic belief that "there is water in copper". If we take a hint from the creation story's use of the water symbol, and look at the atomic structure of copper, we might also make sense of this statement, because like many atoms, the electron structure of copper begins conceptually with two electrons in the innermost electron ring and eight electrons in the second ring–a repetition of the number symbols found in water. So structurally copper "has water in it", just as the Dogon said. Our success in using this same approach to explain the Dogon statement about copper helps to verify that we are on the right track in our understanding of the symbol of water. The inclusion within the creation story of two such similar statements relating to atomic structure provides a kind of self-validation that confirms both interpretations as intended meanings.

We may recall from our earlier discussion about the Sumerian gods An, Enlil, and Enki, the difficulties scholars have faced when trying to categorize these three deities simply as gods of the heavens, the earth, and the waters, respectively, and the persistent link to water that comes into play in their symbolism. We may also recall differences in the symbolism of equivalent deities from culture to culture, as in the case of Enlil, Bel, and Neith, who are in some instances identified as gods or goddesses of the air (conceived as a liquid), others as gods of the atmosphere, and still others as gods of vapor or humidity. But if we step back and take a broader look at the complete triad of gods in any one culture, we quickly realize that as a group they might more aptly be represented as the *three states of water– liquid, solid and vapor.* Our encyclopedic sources tell us that water is the only substance that naturally occurs at normal temperatures in all three of these states liquid, solid and vapor. Since ice is not a substance that would be familiar to the experience of a society living in a sub-tropical area of the world (in fact, Wallis Budge includes no entry in his *Hieroglyphic Dictionary* for the words *ice, freeze,* or *frozen*)–the images of hardened clay and moisture in rocks may have been substituted for ice as the solid form of water. When we test this supposition by applying the meaning of clay to Enki, Ea, and Khnoum, we find that it draws together the divergent images of a god of dryness, a god of the earth, and a god of the waters of the earth in a way that makes complete sense. In a similar way, the assignment of water vapor as the symbol of our goddesses of the air helps us to integrate the symbols of various gods and goddess who are alternately represented by the atmosphere, moisture, and humidity.

Continuing along this same path and using our encyclopedia articles on water as a guide, we would next expect to find somewhere in the creation myths a discussion of the natural water cycle of the earth. In fact, Marcel Griaule devotes portions of chapter 16 of *Conversations With Ogotemmeli* to a discussion of the Dogon understanding of the celestial ram as a symbol for the natural water cycle. To briefly summarize the meanings as the Dogon know them, the calabash between the horns of the ram represents the sun, the horns themselves collect the waters of the rain, the fleece of the ram symbolizes the ground that soaks up the water, and his urine is symbolic of precipitation. When the ram moves among the high clouds, his hooves leave a trail of four colors–black, red, green and yellow–which is the rainbow. As we mentioned earlier, Griaule quotes Ogotemmeli as saying, "To draw up and then return what one had drawn–that is the life of the world." The presence of these symbols in the Dogon creation story, the very ones anticipated by our supposition, and in conjuction with each of the other expected water meanings, shows a degree of intention behind the organization of the myths that goes beyond coincidence.

Now if we return to the original creation story and insert these water-related meanings in place of the corresponding Dogon symbols, the first portion of the myth can be read as a sensible statement about the creation of the universe. In it, the stars are said to be pellets of clay flung out into space by Amma–this is the familiar scenario of the Big Bang theory of modern science. (Pritchard mentions as a note regarding the Egyptian story of the creation of the universe by Atum that, "The creation of Shu . . . and of Tefnut was as explosive as a sneeze.") The art of pottery is established as a metaphor for the act of creating. The stars, which are described as clay pellets thrown out by Amma, represent the original matter of the universe that science tells us coalesced under the influence of gravity to form stars and planets. In this context, the Dogon are correct that the sun is like a pot raised to a high heat–a body of matter massive enough to attain fusion–surrounded by a copper coil with eight turns. Here copper may be used as a metaphor for sunlight to introduce the image of spiraling coils and imply the rotation of the sun. But in fact, modern science actually defines eight separate zones or spheres that comprise the sun–the core, the radiant zone, the convection zone, the photosphere, the sunspots, the magnetic field, the corona and the solar wind. According to Griaule, the Dogon know that the sun is "in some sort a star", a belief that is also in complete agreement with science. Amma created the Nummo, the perfect twin pair which represent hydrogen, the very element that science tells us was the most abundant of the primordial universe along with lesser amounts of oxygen and carbon. The sun's rays are the excrement of the Nummo, which we know is the by-product of the fusion of hydrogen atoms– again in complete agreement with modern science. The Nummo pair with eight members represents water, which the Dogon say is the essence of life, and again science agrees. The Dogon are absolutely correct when they say that the Nummo pair is found in all water, and tell us explicitly that Nummo is water, just as the Egyptians clearly tell us that Nun and Atum are water.

The Dogon believe that at the time of the creation of the earth, the initial conception was flawed because it did not create water. This statement from mythology is supported by many present-day astronomers who feel that the earth at the time of formation did not contain the necessary water to support life. They theorize that the bulk of earth's water was delivered here by comets. This process, just as the Dogon describe it, is akin to an act of fertilization because without water there could be no life on earth. We find a clear presentation of this theory in the October 30th, 1999 edition of **Science News, Vol 156, No. 18**:

> "The origin of terrestrial water has perplexed scientists for decades. Astronomers have proposed that comets, the frozen, water-bearing emigres from the outer solar system, could have delivered much of the Earth's water during the first few hundred million years of the planet's existence. During this epoch, known as the late heavy bombardment, comets pelted the Earth and the other inner planets at a far higher rate than they do today." (*Science News* p. 284)

There are also emerging theories about another process, very much like the Dogon story of Amma's fertilization of the earth, which describes the delivery of organic molecules to the earth by meteor. A summary of the process is presented in the March 25th, 2000 edition of **Science News, Vol 157, No. 13:**

> "A new study shows that carbon molecules known as fullerenes can originate outside the solar system and ride in on meteors. Fullerenes are hollow, spherical molecules made of pure carbon . . . This research

lends support to the idea that organic molecules from space could have played a role in starting the chemical processes necessary for the origin of life." (*Science News*)

So it can be seen from the preceding exercise that if we replace the symbols of the Dogon creation story with basic encyclopedic values relating to water, the result is a statement about the creation of the universe and the creation of the earth that is organized, succinct, and factually correct. Not only are the facts presented just the ones we would expect to find in an encyclopedia article on water, they also appear in the same logical and organized sequence. More importantly, the interpretation that brings us to this conclusion begins by substituting the meaning of water for a symbol that we are emphatically told means water, and ends by validating both the obvious and the enigmatic statements of the Dogon. We could hardly ask for better proof of a supposition.

The next most obvious themes of the Dogon creation story relate to fertilization and the creation of life. Images of intercourse and fertilization appear again and again throughout the myths of each of the civilizations we have discussed. Symbol after symbol is said to represent a woman, her reproductive parts, the divine seed, and so forth. If we review the Dogon creation story again taking the same analytical approach as before, but this time applying meanings to the symbols that relate to fertilization and the creation of life, we find we are rewarded with similarly satisfying results. In this case, Amma represents the first living single-cell, which according to modern science, emerged self-created from the waters of the ancient ocean, described by science as a kind of primordial soup. The perfect Nummo pair are then formed by mitosis, a process defined as the simple asexual division of a cell. This process of splitting results in a matching pair of new cells, each with the same chromosomal makup as the original cell.

The eight ancestors of the Dogon, much like the first eight emergent Egyptian gods and goddesses, could then be seen as an example of the more complicated sexual reproductive process called meiosis. During sexual reproduction, a male and female organism each contribute a germ cell containing only half of the usual number of chromosomes. To do this, two cells–one from each organism–must divide in a way that is unique to the process of meiosis. The result is four germ cells–two from the male and two from the female.

The surface narrative of the Dogon myths tell about the creation of the eight ancestors, the first four of whom are male, the last four female. Looking at this aspect of the story for a moment as a description of the differentiation of germ cells during the process of meiosis, we can see that the formation of the four male and female ancestors is in accordance with the description of cell division during the process of meiosis. Since this method of reproduction applies only to the creation of germ cells, we can now make sense of the Dogon statement that the eight ancestors were allowed to "self-fertilize" by a "special dispensation" granted only to them. We can also understand the statement that the "eight ancestors did not know death" if we consider the relative longevity of the female egg cell, which by comparison with other cells of the body, is essentially immortal, and by the passing-on of genetic information to later generations, a process relating to germ cells which might be seen as a form of true immortality.

The next section of the Dogon creation story can easily be seen as a description of sexual reproduction–in fact, it can hardly be seen as anything but a description of sexual reproduction. The earth has already been established as a metaphor for a woman and we have been told that the anthill represents her sexual organ. The story tells that the eighth ancestor, who symbolizes one of our eight germ cells, descends into the opening of the earth and disappears, all except the hard wooden bowl he wears on his head because it catches on the sides of the opening. This is almost a clinical description of a sperm as it enters the egg at the moment of fertilization, an act that causes the egg to become impenetrable to other sperm. The description of the Nummo as half-man/half-serpent, or as having the head of a fish over the head of a man with the tail of a serpent, is the very image of a sperm cell, and might well be what is pictured in the Egyptian symbol of the Eye of Ra. The very odd story of weaving as introduced by the first transformed ancestor, which involves the interweaving of thin fibers between the teeth of the ancestor, may describe the interweaving of the thin chromosome filaments within the fertilized egg at the time of conception to create a complete new set of DNA. An interesting detail relating to reproduction can be found in the Egyptian creation myth of Hermopolis, in which the eight ancestors are represented by pairs of serpents and frogs who form an egg–in scientific terms a zygote. This detail is echoed by the Dogon concept of the egg of Amma, in which, according to the deep storyline for the Dogon, the original creation was supposed to have occurred. It seems more than appropriate and fitting in what appears to be an allegory about sexual reproduction for germ cells to be represented as ancestors.

A later story about the ancestor smithy, who fires an arrow into the vault of the sky and forms a spindle, is also a likely reference to asexual reproduction, which is the growth process that continues after the sperm and egg join. During this process, a spindle or scaffold is formed, along which the chromosomes move as they separate in two halves at opposite ends of the cell, in preparation for the cell to divide.

The Dogon describe this journey of the eighth ancestor as entering the womb of the earth, and it is a journey that each of the eight ancestors must take in series during the process of transformation, just as the eight germ cells presumably take their reproductive journeys of transformation. Once inside the womb, the eighth ancestor gains knowledge of the Word of the female Nummo, which with the help of the male Nummo, takes the shape of a spiraling coil and is transmitted via the womb. This spiraling coil is the textbook image of the DNA molecule with its spiraling coils–the double-helix–which we know is the medium of transmission of the genetic word. The Dogon are again correct that this transmission can only come about with the help of both the female and the male partners. Based on this interpretation of the story we now understand one reason for the repeat emphasis placed by the Dogon creation story on spiraling coil symbols, and the references within the myth to the idea of the word being woven into the cloth, because the chromosomes of DNA are the genetic words that are literally woven into the fabric of each cell. Finally, the story tells us that the eighth ancestor takes fetal form and undergoes an extended period of transformation, which again accurately reflects the next step in the reproductive process, the period of gestation. Each of these images is completely in accordance with what we know from science about the process of sexual reproduction and is presented in a form that could hardly relate to anything but sexual reproduction. So again, this second effort to assign meaning to the Dogon creation symbols results in an organized, factual and understandable statement about the creation of life and sexual reproduction that is in complete agreement with what a modern encyclopedia would tell us.

In support of this line of interpretation, Griaule and Dieterlen carefully relate to us some of the sophisticated aspects of Dogon thought as it relates to the reproductive process:

"The children have . . . the same seeds as their par-

> ents: those of the father are in a dominant position
> for a boy and those of the mother for a girl; eight in
> number and of different "sex", the boy first inherits
> the "masculine seeds" from his father, which are the
> same as those of his [male] ancestors, and the daugh-
> ter the "feminine seeds" of her mother, which are
> the same as those of her uterine ancestors. Thus, in a
> symbolism of a biological nature the presence of a
> double filiation is delineated." (*The Pale Fox* p. 54)

The third theme of the Dogon myths is that of the creation of civilization and is found at the narrative level of the
story itself. This storyline describes in an organized fashion
each of the skills needed to bring a populace of hunter/
gatherers to the level of an agrarian society. To briefly review, these skills are:

- Spoken and written language.
- The concept of clothing.
- The art of weaving.
- The art of pottery.
- The skills of agriculture.
- The skills of metallurgy for making the tools of
  agriculture.
- A basic family structure.
- A basic framework for community.
- The skills to construct dwellings and storage
  facilities.

In this aspect of the story, the key creation symbols are
used as mnemonic devices, rather than objects of symbolic
meaning. As the narrative progresses, each new skill is presented using the same set of symbols previously defined in
the myths, and each skill is carefully equated with those
previously learned. For example, the movement of the shuttle
across the warp during the act of weaving is said to be the

same as the motion of the plow across the field when discussing agriculture. At the same time, the processes required for mastery of each skill are represented symbolically in the form of commonly-found objects, such as the woven garment that a person wears, the configuration of a plowed field, or the granary around which a community is centered. In this way, the trappings of daily life serve as constant reminders of the civilizing skills that have been learned. The Dogon creation myth presents these skills–an arguably correct set of skills–in an orderly and organized sequence, much the same sequence as they may actually have been acquired by mankind.

Taken together, these three stories-within-a-story of the Dogon creation myth provide a full and accurate account of the formative processes that brought mankind to a level of civilized consciousness–just what one would expect to find in a deliberate telling of a story of creation. If true, the meanings as we have assigned them to the symbols reveal a document that is instructional in nature, a text that of itself could reasonably be interpreted as taught knowledge. And although this kind of an interpretation might seem far-fetched, it is one that is actually supported by the ancient myths themselves, since many of the oldest written texts say and most early societies clearly believed that the skills of civilization were taught to mankind. So the pursuit of this line of reasoning is actually in accordance with what the original texts state. Modern science, however, interprets the surviving documents of these early societies as a blending of mythology and history, and so all such statements have been assigned to the realm of the mythological. But over the course of the past two centuries, the imaginary line that separates ancient mythology from ancient history has moved slowly and persistently backward in time as each new archeological discovery causes us to understand as historic what was formerly thought to be mythic.

Chapter 5: The Big Bang, Atomic & Quantum Structure

The preceding discussion demonstrates many superficial resemblances between the surface narrative of the Dogon creation story and the Big Bang theory of science. But Marcel Griaule and Germaine Dieterlen maintain that one of the primary functions of the surface storyline of the Dogon is to serve as a kind of mask for a more detailed body of knowledge contained within the deep storyline. Therefore, if we are to believe that we are on the right track with our interpretation of Dogon symbols from the surface storyline, we should expect to find even more specific and recognizable details of the Big Bang theory incorporated into the deep storyline. And in fact, when we carefully examine the elements of the deep storyline, this is exactly what we find.

For the Dogon, the starting point for the deep storyline is *Amma's egg*–the mythological counterpart of the unformed universe that contained all of the seeds or signs of the world. According to Dogon mythology, it was the opening of this egg that created all of the spiraling galaxies of stars and worlds. This concept of the origin of the universe conforms nicely to the prevailing theories of astrophysics, which define the unformed universe prior to the Big Bang as a kind of ball containing all of the potential matter of the future universe compressed to an unbelievably dense state. Accordingly, it was the rupturing of this ball that ultimately scattered matter as we now know it to the farthest reaches of the universe. Rush W. Dozier, Jr. describes the modern conception of the unformed universe in *Codes of Evolution*:

" . . . every form of matter, life and thought that exists today can trace its ancestry through a sequence of earlier forms all the way back to the big bang. The big bang, the echo of which we can still detect as the sea of microwave radiation that fills the universe, is the common ancestor of all things. Evolution began with the big bang. It created space, time, matter, and change: the basic ingredients of unified selection.

The theories of physics suggest that until the big bang there was no space and time as we comprehend the terms. There was no distinction between present and past, and all particles and forces merged into a single, primal field.

The perfect unity that existed at the moment of the big bang has unraveled over the eons. Since the big bang, the overall direction of change in the universe has been one-way: from order to chaos." (*Codes of Evolution* p. 7-8)

As is the case with many of their religious concepts, the Dogon make use of a tangible figure to help them visualize their unformed universe–a carved stone that symbolizes the original primordial egg. Griaule and Dieterlen describe this stone in a passage from **The Pale Fox**:

"This conception of creation is recalled by a figure of the 266 primordial signs schematically drawn under a raised stone . . . The stone is carved into a slight point (in the form of an egg); it is quadrangular, the corners marking the cardinal directions of the future "opening of Amma's egg"." (*The Pale Fox* p. 101 and 105)

This physical representation of Amma's egg–a stone with tapered sides that come almost to a point–is reminiscent of the shape of the Dogon granary: conical yet roughly pyramidal. The egg also serves a kind of parallel function to the granary. Just as Amma's egg holds the seeds of the future world, so the Dogon granary holds the seeds of the eight grains of the Dogon. So both in physical appearance and in function, the granary might be thought of as an alternate rendering of Amma's egg.

According to most astronomers, the "perfect unity that existed at the moment of the big bang"–science's equivalent of Amma's egg–represented a singularity, most like what we now know as a black hole. Stephen Hawking describes the concept of a black hole in the following way in *A Brief History of Time*:

> " . . . John Michell wrote a paper in 1783 in the *Philosophical Transactions of the Royal Society of London* in which he pointed out that a star that was sufficiently massive and compact would have such a strong gravitational field that light could not escape; any light emitted from the surface of the star would be dragged back by the star's gravitational attraction before it could get very far . . . Such objects are what we now call black holes, because that is what they are: black voids in space . . .
>
> According to the theory of relativity, nothing can travel faster than light. Thus if light cannot escape, neither can anything else; everything is dragged back by the gravitational field. So one has a set of events, a region of space-time, from which it is not possible to escape to reach a distant observer . . . Its boundary is called the event horizon and coincides with the paths of light rays that just fail to escape from the black hole." (*A Brief History Of Time* p. 81-86)

The diagram provided by Hawking to describe this *event horizon*–the path of the light rays that are unable to leave the black hole–is in most respects the very image of the Dogon stone representing *Amma's egg* :

Hawking's Diagram

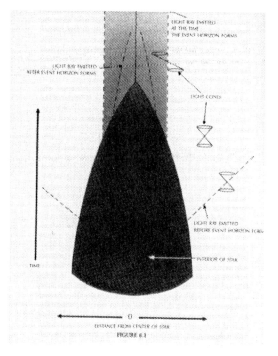

Dogon Rendering of Amma's Egg

In many early mythologies, the original creation of the universe is linked to the opening of an egg, much like the egg of the Dogon. The first entities to emerge after the moment of creation are the familiar triad of gods that we previously associated with the three physical states of water. Scientists believe that the plasma that emerged from the Big Bang was intensely hot, and cooled rapidly to the near-zero temperature that we now see in the vacuum of space. In a recent article in the August 26th, 2000 issue of **Science News** entitled **Seeking the Mother of all Matter**, this cooling process and its effect on the matter of space is described:

> "Even as RHIC experiments probe the tiniest volumes of space, they also may help scientists make more sense of the biggest thing there is – the universe. As a quark-gluon plasma cools, it condenses into hadrons. This occurs because the inwardly directed pressure of the zero-temperature plasma has taken over, forcing the plasma's constituents back into protons and neutrons. Physicists regard that condensation as a phase transition, like steam becoming water or water freezing into ice." (Science News Vol. 158, No. 9, p. 138)

Prevailing astronomic theory explains that the first finished by-product of this cooling process after the Big Bang was the atom, and more specifically the hydrogen atom–the Dogon surface storyline's counterpart to the Nummo. Again, if our understanding of the structure of the Dogon religion is correct, we would expect the deep creation storyline to include specific information about the atom and its constituent components, and again in fact it does. We find information about the atom in a section of **The Pale Fox** entitled "Creation of the Po". For the Dogon, the *po* is the name of the "smallest grain", and represents one of the tiniest building blocks of the universe:

"Thus, inside the egg Amma himself was like a spiraling motion, called "accelerated ball," *ogoni gunnu;* then the oval *po* seed was created, which placed itself invisibly at the center. It is said: "When Amma broke the egg of the world and came out, a whirlwind rose. The *po*, which is the smallest (thing), was made, invisible at the center; the wind is Amma himself. It is the *po* which Amma let come out first." Amma's creative will was located in the *po*, the smallest of things. Like a central air bubble, it spun and scattered the particles of matter in a sonorous and luminous motion which, however, remained inaudible and invisible. It was less a word than a thought . . . the *po* is the image of the origin of matter. Therefore, it will later be forbidden for different categories of men to . . . speak about it; because "the beginning of things is Amma's greatest secret." Moreover, the *po* is also the image of the creator. "Amma, the creator, was not himself great (big), but of that it is forbidden to speak . . . Amma, from the moment when he created all things, each was like the *po*; they grew larger whereas the *po* did not; the seed was formed like the wind and it is forbidden to talk about it."

The seed is . . . called *po*, a word considered to have the same root as p*olo*, "beginning". Indeed, due to its smallness, it is the image of the beginning of all things. "All of the things that Amma created begin like the little (seed of) *po*." And, beginning with this infinitely small thing, the things created by Amma will form themselves by continuous addition of identical elements; "Amma makes things begin (by creating them as) small (as the) *po*; he continues to add (to the things created) little by little . . . As Amma adds . . . the thing becomes large." (*The Pale Fox* p. 130-131)

Dogon descriptions of the *po* at the opening of *Amma's egg*, forming like a central air bubble and scattering in a luminous motion, correlate well with scientific descriptions of the process of cooling of the quark-gluon plasma. If we read on further in the same **Science News** article, it states:

> "It is common during phase transitions, like water's familiar ones, for bubbles of unchanged matter to linger and then suddenly and violently burst in a belated transformation into the new phase."

Clearly what is being spoken of in the above passages is the formation of the building blocks of matter–atoms and their components. So when we suggest possible meanings for the Dogon symbols that are related to atomic structure, the idea is wholly and completely in keeping with how the Dogon understand their own symbols. But if we look carefully, we can see that the surface story of the Dogon may also pointedly direct us to the concepts of quantum physics. Imagine for a moment that you must read an article written in a foreign language which, for the most part, you do not understand. And imagine again that two words you do understand–*supply* and *demand* are repeated again and again within the passage. It would not take the insight of a genius to surmise that the subject of the article might be economics. The Dogon creation story provides us with a similar clue to its meaning with its recurring emphasis on pellets of clay and spiraling coils. It requires only a little imagination to see these symbols as likely references to *particles* and *waves*– the essential building blocks of quantum theory. We find a good description of this dual nature of quantum particles in Richard P. Feynman's **The Character of Physical Law**:

> "Electrons, when they were first discovered, behaved exactly like particles or bullets, very simply. Further research showed, from electron diffraction experi-

ments for example, that they behaved like waves.
As time went on there was a growing confusion about
how these things really behaved—waves or particles,
particles or waves? Everything looked like both."
"This growing confusion was resolved in 1925 or
1926 with the advent of correct equations for quantum mechanics. Now we know how the electrons
and light behave. But what can I call it? If I say they
behave like particles, I give the wrong impression;
also if I say they behave like waves. They behave in
their own inimitable way, which technically could be
called a quantum mechanical way." (*The Character
of Physical Law* p. 128)

Within the creation story we can see an implied knowledge of the wave properties of physics when the Dogon
say that the fibers of the first garment mimic the sound of
the voice of the Nummo as it tapers off—a statement which
betrays an understanding by the creation story's teller that
sound travels in waves.

If we look more deeply into the subject of quantum
physics, we learn about a fundamental principle, called *the
exclusion principle*, which states that no two electrons can
occupy the same quantum or energy state of an atom at the
same time. The quantum state of an electron is defined by
four mathematical values called *quantum numbers*. So if we
return to our first interpretation of the Dogon creation story
in which the Nummo pair represent the electrons of hydrogen, the science of quantum physics brings us right back to
our same Dogon number symbols, two and eight—which in
this case represent the two electrons and their eight quantum numbers. A little further inquiry into the subject tells us
that not only electrons but also protons and neutrons in the
nucleus of an atom are bound by a fundamental limit that
allows only two per quantum orbit, and those two must be
of opposite spins. These requirements of science speak to

two fundamental notions of the Dogon creation story–the principle in the universe of twin births and the inherent pairing of male and female, in this instance represented as positive and negative.

The next key concept of quantum physics that we should examine is Heisenberg's *uncertainty principle*, which declares that it is not possible to know the exact position and momentum of an electron at the same instant. The reason for this is that physicists learn about the nature of quantum particles through inference by deliberately bouncing other particles off them. But because these particles are so very small and lightweight, any collision with another particle will necessarily disturb their position or momentum. Consequently, a scientist can determine the precise position of a quantum particle or its precise momentum, but not both at the same moment.

Unlikely as it may seem, this principle of quantum physics brings us to an interesting puzzle relating both to the granary and the pyramid. Among the ancient civilizations of the world, we find two basic types of pyramids–those with flat tops and those that come to a peak. We can find examples of both varieties of pyramid among the symbols of the Egyptian religion, while in Dogon mythology we are told only about the flat-topped granary. But there is an unusual discrepancy within the Dogon mythology itself pertaining to the granary and its physical shape. The Dogon creation myth provides us with specific dimensions for the structure of the granary, including a round base with a diameter of 20 cubits, four 10-step staircases (one per side) with steps measuring one cubit high and one cubit deep, rising to a square, flat top measuring 8 cubits per side. But when we actually apply these dimensions to a model in which the steps are inset as part of the face (as would be the case with a step-pyramid), we are left with a basic contradiction in the dimensions.

If we restrict ourselves to a base with a diameter of 20

cubits, four stairways with ten 1-cubit steps would meet at nearly a peak, leaving a square of only 2 cubits per side at the top of the granary. In order to build a model with a square flat top of sides measuring 8 cubits, we would either have to reduce the number of steps to 6 per side, or else move the base of each stairway several cubits out from the circular edge of the granary. In other words, we can place the staircases in the right location or include the correct number of steps, but not both. This quandary is of precisely the same nature as the uncertainty principle of the quantum theory, and expresses itself mathematically in terms of the number of steps in four staircases, the same as the number of values needed to define the quantum state of an electron.

In *The Pale Fox*, Griaule and Dieterlen describe a basic approach to the act of creating that is defined within the framework of Dogon mythology. This approach includes four phases or steps and, for the Dogon, applies equally to any creative project, whether it be a creative act of Amma or an undertaking of man–for example, the building of a dwelling place. The first of these is the conceptual stage, in which an idea is conceived, and which the Dogon call *bummo*. At this stage, the project exists only in signs or seeds–symbols that represent the final thing to be created. For a middle school student assigned to write a report, this would be the equivalent of selecting a topic. The second stage, called the *yala*, conceptualizes the project in broad strokes whose purpose is to identify the boundaries of the created object. This compares roughly to our middle school student's report outline. Griaule and Dieterlen describe this phase in *The Pale Fox*:

> " . . . after the first series, that of abstract signs or "trace" *bummo* will come the second series, that of the *yala* "mark" or "image", executed in dotted lines . . . The *yala* of a thing is like the beginning of the thing."

Therefore, when one builds a house, one delineates the foundation with stones placed at the corners: these stones are the *yala*, the "marks" of the future dwelling. The term *yala* also has the meaning of "reflection", which expresses the future form of the thing represented." (*The Pale Fox* p. 95)

The third developmental stage refines the image of the thing to be created by filling in the main details of the object or concept. We could say that this third stage would be comparable to a student's detailed notes, or perhaps to a first draft of the report. In regard to this stage, Griaule and Dieterlen write:

"The third series of signs is that of the *tonu*, "figure", "diagram," or sometimes "periphery," of things. The *tonu* is a schematic outline of generally separated graphic elements; it is the sketch, the rough draft of the thing or being represented. The word *tonu* comes from *tono*, "to portray," which also means "to begin," but in the dynamic sense of the word. It is said that Amma "began things", *amma kize tono*, to demonstrate the initial impetus he gave to creation . . . The *tonu* of the house connotes the pebbles that have been placed between the corner- stones to delimit the walls." (*The Pale Fox* p. 95-96)

The fourth and final stage of the creative act is to produce the finished image of the thing to be created. It is interesting that the Dogon make almost no distinction between the representation of an object and the object itself. Griaule and Dieterlen say of this completion stage:

"The fourth series consists of the "drawings", *toymu* (or *toy*), as realistically representative of the thing as possible. It is also the thing itself. When one has finished the building of a house, it is as if one had made a complete drawing, *toymu*, of the house. In speaking of the *toy* and of Amma, one says: "To make the drawing is to make the thing that he (Amma) has in mind. It is, therefore, to represent the thing created in its reality." (*The Pale Fox* p. 95-96)

The example of building a house is an interesting one for Griaule and Dieterlen to have selected to illustrate the creative process, because it reveals the creation myth as a likely source of architectural knowledge. In fact, the four-step process from *bummo* to *yala* to *tonu* to *toy* is very similar to the process taught to modern students of architectural drawing–first conceiving the structure, then defining with point-marks the outer boundaries of a structure, then marking in greater detail the other structural features, and finally creating the finished drawing. Likewise it is similar to the usual modern approach to construction itself, in which a site is surveyed, oriented and staked before any actual construction work begins. But most importantly, it represents a basic organizational mindset of the sort needed for any person or culture to advance successfully.

As we examine the Dogon symbols as they relate to quantum physics, we should note that the four creative stages of the Dogon–*bummo, yala, tonu and toy*–may have bearing on another set of concepts from quantum physics relating to the four types of force-carrying particles. Stephen Hawking describes these particles and their relationship to the building blocks of atoms in **A Brief History of Time:**

"Force-carrying particles can be grouped into four categories according to the strength of the force that they carry and the particles with which they interact . . . The first category is the gravitational force. This force is universal, that is, every particle feels the force of gravity, according to its mass or energy . . .

the force between two matter particles is pictured as
being carried by a particle . . . called the graviton . . .
gravitons . . . are very weak–and so difficult to detect that they have never yet been observed."

"The next category is the electromagnetic force,
which interacts with electrically charged particles like
electrons . . . The electromagnetic attraction between
negatively charged electrons and positively charged
protons in the nucleus causes the electrons to orbit
the nucleus of the atom . . . ."

"The third category is called the weak nuclear
force . . . [this force] exhibits a property known as
spontaneous symmetry breaking. This means that
what appear to be a number of completely different
particles at low energies are in fact found to be all
the same type of particle, only in different states . . .
The effect is rather like the behaviour of a roulette
ball on a roulette wheel. At high energies (when the
wheel is spun quickly) the ball behaves essentially in
only one way–it rolls round and round.

But as the wheel slows, the energy of the ball de-
creases, and eventually the ball drops into one of the
thirty-seven slots in the wheel."

"The fourth category is the strong nuclear force,
which holds the quarks together in the proton and
neutron, and holds the protons and neutrons together
in the nucleus of the atom." (*A Brief History of Time*
p. 69-72)

These particles as Hawking describes them follow the
same pattern as the *bummo, yala, tonu and toy*–the graviton
is so weak and undetectable as to be a concept. The electromagnetic force defines the outline of the object. The weak
nuclear force at high energy states refines the component
particles into an approximation of one particle, and the strong
nuclear force binds, or "draws" the atom.

According to the Dogon, the *po* seed–already one of the most basic elements of creation–consists of four even more elemental components, referred to in combination as *the sene seed*. Graiule and Dieterlen say:

> "In this infinitely small thing Amma then placed the four elements which thus far had contained the four *tonu* of the *sene* . . . The *sene* represents the first thing created by Amma . . . Amma's acts are represented by a series of figures. The first, called "diagram of the *sene seed* . . . " connotes the superposition of the four elements in the formation of the seed . . . In accordance with Amma's will, each of them extended its "germ" to touch its neighbor, from east to north, from north to west, etc. This "crossing of the germs" is compared to the intertwining of twigs forming a "nest", *senu*. These germs then gathered at the center, where they mixed together and were transformed at the very site of the *po*, which was still invisible. Then, surrounding the seed, they made it visible . . ." (*The Pale Fox* p. 132-134)

This "crossing of the germs" in all directions is a very competent description aimed at a non-technical observer of the electrons in their crossing orbits surrounding an atom. These orbiting electrons, combined with their nucleus–the *po*–comprise a completed atom.

Graiule and Dieterlen present as a figure within *The Pale Fox*, a Dogon diagram of the *sene seed* that is a close match for typical scientific diagrams showing normal electron density and electron orbital shapes. Compare the scientific diagram reproduced below with the Dogon drawing beneath it as rendered in *The Pale Fox*:

Electron Orbit Shape

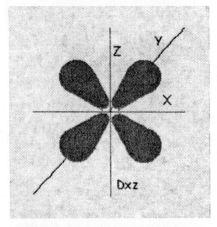

Dogon Drawing of the Sene

The shape of the electron orbit diagram is based on mathematical calculations of the most probable location of electrons as they orbit around a nucleus. But the shape of the orbit itself is far from being theoretical, since it has been verified by many scientific experiments and validated by actual images produced by electron microscopes.

Based on this interpretation, the *sene* of the Dogon would represent components of an atom: electrons, protons and neutrons. But the Dogon also speak about the *germination of the sene,* which from this point of view would mean the creation of electrons, protons and neutrons from smaller particles. What this suggests is that, for us to understand the Dogon symbols for the *germination of the sene,* it could only be helpful to know more about these particles. So for this explanation, we turn again to the comments of Stephen Hawking in *A Brief History of Time*:

> "Using the wave/particle duality . . . everything in the universe, including light and gravity, can be described in terms of particles. These particles have a property called spin. One way of thinking of spin is to imagine the particles as little tops spinning about an axis. However, this can be misleading, because quantum mechanics tells us that the particles do not have any well-defined axis. What the spin of a particle really tells us is what the particle looks like from different directions. A particle of spin 0 . . . looks the same from every direction. On the other hand, a particle of spin 1 is like an arrow: it looks different from different directions. Only if one turns it round a complete revolution (360 degrees) does the particle look the same. A particle of spin 2 is like a double-headed arrow: it looks the same if one turns it round half a revolution (180 degrees) . . . but the remarkable fact is that there are particles that do not look the same if one turns them through just one revolution: you have to turn them through two complete revolutions! Such particles are said to have a spin of 1/2. (*A Brief History Of Time* p. 66-67)"

The above description by Hawking from quantum physics provides us with an exceptionally workable caption for the Dogon diagram of *the germination of the sene,* also taken from *The Pale Fox:*

Germination of the Sene

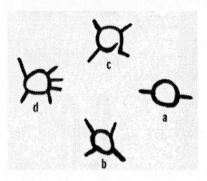

Figure (b) in the above diagram represents Hawking's particle with a spin value of 0–based on *four cardinal points,* it looks the same from all perspectives. Figure (c) represents a particle with a spin value of 1–it must be turned 360 degrees in order to look the same. Figure (a) corresponds to a particle with a spin value of 2–it needs only be turned 180 degrees to look the same. The very odd layout of figure (d) is an attempt–obviously not possible in two dimensions– to represent a particle with a spin value of 1/2–requiring two full 360 degree turns to look the same. In relation to these particles, Hawking also tells us:

> "All the known particles in the universe can be di-
> vided into two groups: particles of spin 1/2, which
> make up the matter in the universe, and particles of
> spin 0, 1 and 2, which . . . give rise to forces between
> the matter particles." (*A Brief History of Time* p. 67)

Although the Dogon diagram is unable to accurately portray the 1/2 spin particle, the author of the Dogon creation story came up with an inventive way of describing it, once again using the symbol of the granary–the same symbol previously used to represent concepts of quantum physics. This interpretation begins with the assignment of a set of values to the *sene* particles which reaffirm their identification as the components of matter of all variety. Griaule and Dieterlen write in *The Pale Fox*:

> "Having thought and then designed the world he wished to create, Amma tried as an experiment to superimpose a bit of every kind of substance . . . The result of this first labor was the seed of the tree *sene na* . . . The oval-shaped seed . . . had to contain four elements . . . It is said that in order to create the *sene na*, Amma "cleared his throat, which made earth; his saliva became water; he breathed when he returned to the sky, this being fire; he blew hard, this being wind. He did not mix the elements, but superposed them: he put down earth, then water, then fire, then air. "Amma, to create the *sene na*," superposed things separated into four. (*The Pale Fox* p.110)

In this way, the symbolic interpretation was assigned that all matter is created from the four elements of *earth, water, fire and wind*–symbols actually associated with the four types of quantum particles, but later apparently mistaken by the Greeks to be the actual components of all matter. Based on this symbolism, we now understand that when Dogon mythology speaks of fire, it may actually be in reference to a quantum particle. This knowledge provides us with the necessary key to understand the otherwise obscure Dogon tale of the stolen fire of the smithy–a tale that demonstrates that the Greeks knew of these same symbols because of its parallels to the Greek myth of Prometheus, who was said to have stolen fire from the gods. Marcel Griaule relates this story in *Conversations With Ogotemmeli*:

> "All was now ready . . . except that there was no fire in the smithy. The ancestor slipped into the workshop of the great Nummo, who are Heaven's smiths,

and stole a piece of the sun in the form of live embers and white-hot iron. He seized it by means of a 'robbers stick' the crook of which ended in a slit, open like a mouth. He dropped some of the embers, came back to pick them up, and fled towards the granary; but his agitation was such that he could no longer find the entrances. He made the round of it several times before he found the steps and climbed to the flat roof, where he hid the stolen goods in one of the skins of the bellows, exclaiming: *'Gouyo!'*, which is to say, 'Stolen!'" (*Conversations With Ogotemmeli* p. 42)

On the surface, this story makes absolutely no sense, since we know that the granary had four staircases to the top, so the ancestor should not have had to circle it even once to find steps to the top. But we know from the symbolism of the sene that fire is the symbol of a quantum element from which all matter is made, which Hawking tells us is the 1/2 spin particle. The act of circling the granary more than once to get back to the start is a reference to the double-turn (720 degrees) required to return the 1/2 spin particle back to its starting point. The symbolism of the word "stolen" is a reference to electrons–a sub-particle made from the 1/2 spin particle, and the one that science tells us is stolen from one atom by another in order to form a molecular bond. Furthermore, Hawking tells us:

"Modern nuclear theory is based on the notion that nuclei consist of neutrons and protons that are held together by extremely powerful "nuclear" forces. The elucidation of these nuclear forces requires physicists to disrupt neutrons and protons by bombarding nuclei with extremely energetic particles. Such bombardments have revealed more than 200 so-called elementary particles, or tiny bits of matter, most of which exist for much less than one hundred-millionth of a second." (*A Brief History of Time* p.)

When Hawking speaks of the existence of "more than 200" elementary particles, he implies that there are more types of particles to be found, as yet undiscovered or unconfirmed by modern science. This approximate number of particles correlates well with the Dogon figure of 266 seeds or signs. Griaule and Dieterlen go on to tell us that these 266 signs are classified into alternate groupings by the Dogon:

"Moreover, Amma's 266 *bummo*, of which we have seen the basic division into 8, are also classified in the following manner: 6, then 20, then 4 times 60. During the sowing celebration, when the sacrifice is offered on the altar called *manna amma*, "Amma of the sky", the Arou priest says: "Amma's number is 266; it begins with 6 *bummo* to which are added 20; 4 times 60 more; Amma made 6 *bummo* of things in the beginning; he added 20 (then)placed 4 times 60 more (*bummo*). These two ways denote a division in base 8, female, and a division in base 6, male. This expresses that the *bummo*, symbol of Amma's creative thought, contains in essence–by the specific value of the number, another fundamental expression of the groundwork of creation–sexual twinness, male and female, which will be at the base of the realization in matter of divine thought." (*The Pale Fox* p. 93)

The beginning 6 *bummo* of *Amma's* creation, already identified among the 266 signs as quantum particles, are easily recognized as the 6 varieties of quarks as described by Hawking:

"There are a number of different varieties of quarks: there are thought to be at least six "flavors", which we call up, down, strange, charmed, bottom, and top. Each flavor comes in three "colors", red, green and blue. (It should be emphasized that these terms are just labels; quarks are much smaller than the wavelength of visible light and so do not have any color in the normal sense. It is just that modern physicists seem to have more imaginative ways of naming new particles and phenomena–they no longer restrict themselves to Greek!) A proton or neutron is made up of three quarks, one of each color. A proton contains two up quarks and one down quark; a neutron contains two down quarks and one up." (*A Brief History of Time* p. 65)

Based on the preceding diagrams and Hawkings descriptions of the elemental particles and forces involved with quantum mechanics, we can see that the Dogon deep storyline symbolism relating to the 266 signs or seeds of Amma presents a stunningly accurate portrait of the component building blocks of matter as we presently know them. On the other hand, if the Dogon count of 266 elements ultimately turns out to be the correct scientific number, then the Dogon creation story may well have drawn the meanings of its symbols from a body of scientific knowledge that actually goes a bit beyond our own.

Chapter 6: String Theory

Given the extraordinary correspondence between the Dogon symbols of the *po* and the *sene* to their counterparts within the basic quantum theory, it makes sense to pursue this correspondence one level deeper by examining the structure of the quantum particles themselves. To make this comparison, we must look to the theory of *superstrings*, a promising but as-yet unverifiable theory of what may be the last indivisible component particles of matter. String theory came to the forefront of scientific thought in the early 1980's, and although verification of certain key aspects of the theory remain beyond our technological grasp, it continues to be the most viable candidate for a unified theory of the universe. Brian Greene explains the basis of the theory in his 1999 book ***The Elegant Universe***:

> "[Quantum] particles are the "letters" of all matter. Just like their linguistic counterparts, they appear to have no further internal substructure. String theory proclaims otherwise. According to string theory, if we could examine these particles with even greater precision–a precision many orders of magnitude beyond our present technological capacity–we would find that each is not pointlike, but instead consists of a tiny one dimensional *loop*. Like an infinitely thin rubber band, each particle contains a vibrating, oscillating, dancing filament that physicists . . . have named a *string* . . ." (p. 14)
>
> "[In string theory,] all properties of the microworld are within the realm of its explanatory power. To

understand this, let's first think about more familiar strings, such as those on a violin. Each such string can undergo a huge variety (in fact, infinite in number) of different vibrational patterns known as *resonances* . . . These are the wave patterns whose peaks and troughs are evenly spaced and fit perfectly between the string's two fixed endpoints. Our ears sense the different resonant vibrational patterns as different musical notes.

The strings in string theory have similar properties. There are resonant vibrational patterns that the string can support by virtue of their evenly spaced peaks and troughs exactly fitting along its spacial extent . . . Just as the different vibrational patterns of a violin string give rise to different musical notes, *the different vibrational patterns of a fundamental string give rise to the different masses and force charges.*" (*The Elegant Universe* p. 143)

As a visual aid to understanding strings, Greene includes diagrams of several of these vibrational patterns, one of which is presented below:

Vibrational Pattern of a Quantum String

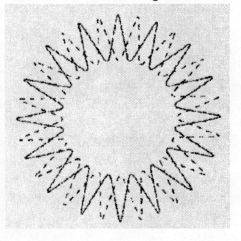

As we continue with our interpretation of the Dogon symbols that would correspond to these quantum strings, we realize that any discussion of components more funda mental than the germination of the sene brings us to the level of the 266 seeds or signs of Amma. In regard to these signs, Marcel Griaule states in his article **The Dogon** that the Dogon "conception of the universe is based . . . on a principle of vibrations of matter . . . .". This basis for the Dogon structure of matter is reaffirmed by a Dogon drawing that describes the 266 seeds or signs. Griaule and Dieterlen tell us again in **The Pale Fox**:

> "The creation and the picture of the signs are also commemorated annually before sowing (*bado*) by the following ritual. Early in the morning the head of the family goes to the "field of the ancestors", v*ageu minne*, and clears a neat area at the center for making the signs.
>
> On this spot he then places a *tazu* basket upside down to draw a circle, which will bear the same name as the altar of the field: then he makes a pile of stones, *sogo*. Facing the east, he first draws on the ground a small circle about 12 cm. in diameter inside the first circle, with a dot in the center. In the course of that day, he makes a zigzag line around the inner circle, repeating this twenty-two times, so as to fill the outer circle with an intricate tangle of lines representing all possible signs . . .
>
> One says of this gesture: "The 266 (signs) are drawn in the center of the field of the ancestors."" (*The Pale Fox* p. 108)

In place of a photograph of this field drawing, Griaule and Dieterlen present what they call a "theoretical diagram" of this drawing, which compares favorably with Greene's vibrational examples:

Dogon Field Drawing

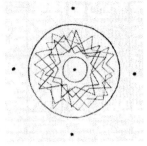

Together, the Dogon field drawing along with Marcel Griaule's statement about the vibrational nature of matter firmly link the subject matter of the Dogon symbols to that of their string-theory counterparts. We know that quantum science assigns the source of these vibrations of matter to the quantum string. It is therefore significant that, for the Dogon, the component structure which would equate to a quantum string is a *thread*, one which is said to be the work of *the spider of the sene*. Griaule and Dieterlen write:

> "Now the spider *dada yurugu geze gezene* (literally: " *dada*" who holds the thread of the Fox") had been delegated by Amma . . . it entered the *sene na..* in order to "weave the words" of Ogo." (*The Pale Fox* p. 236)

Although a quantum string is many times smaller than the smallest particle that can be imaged by present-day technology, the Dogon retain a clear sense of what their quantum thread looks like. Griaule and Dieterlen include the following Dogon diagram of the "work of the spider in the sene" in an appendix to **The Pale Fox**:

Work of the Spider in the *Sene*

Based on the preceding discussion, we can see a continued correlation between Dogon symbols and the deep theoretical science of string theory. But in this one instance, the drawing of the Dogon thread presents us with a significant difference between what science proposes as theory and what the Dogon state as fact: The Dogon tell us that the underlying strings of matter are found in coils, not in loops.

Dogon mythology provides us with other important similarities that help to confirm the identification of the thread of the Dogon spider and the quantum strings of science. For one, just as the strings of string theory are thought to give rise to the four quantum forces–gravity, the electromagnetic force, the weak nuclear force, and the strong nuclear force–the Dogon tell us that the spider of the sene also "gives birth" to *four sene seeds.*

> "The four branches of the *sene na* in which the spider was working will bear fruit . . . The first seed caught by the *sene* was that of the *mono,* a word meaning "to bring together" . . . [the second] *sene gommuzu* or "bumpy"; *sene benu* or "stocky"; *sene urio* that bows (its head). The four *sene* will embody on earth the four *yala* allocated to the *sene na* seed in Amma's womb, which contained the four elements in this order: sene na, water; *sene gommuzo,* air; *sene benu,* fire; *sene urio,* earth." (*The Pale Fox* p. 236-237)

While quantum strings produce what traditional science sees as quantum particles, the thread of the spider of the sene "gives birth" to our four previously-identified categories of quantum spin particles. Many of the specific attributes of string theory vary, depending upon how likely we assume a single string is to split apart, or two strings are to join into one. This likelihood is defined by a numerical value called the *string coupling constant.* The lower the value of the constant, the more strings behave like one-dimensional threads. The higher the value, the more they behave like two dimensional membranes. Brian Greene writes:

> " . . . the fundamental ingredient of the theory appears to be a one- dimensional string . . . however . . . if we . . . turn the value of the respective string coupling constants up . . . what appeared to be one-dimensional strings stretch into two-dimensional membranes." (*The Elegant Universe* p. 315)

According to Griaule and Dieterlen, the spiraling components of matter exhibit similar behavior within the Dogon structure of matter. In a chapter of **The Pale Fox** entitled "The Work of the Po Pilu", they tell us:

> " . . . the spiral of things that were rolled up in the *po* . . . represent the name given by Amma. The names were first put inside the *po*; while whirling about, it created a bond between one thing and the thing after it. In this way, the names formed a sort of thin covering (compared to the one surrounding the brain); by spinning around, this "skin" became like a tube containing things in series." (p. 417)

One version of current string theory, called M-theory, defines a universe that consists of 11 dimensions–four that we can detect (height, width, length and time), and seven that we cannot detect. A good example to help conceptualize one of these undetectable dimensions–borrowed from Brian Greene's **The Elegant Universe**, is to imagine an ant walking across a high-tension power line. From a distance, the power line seems to have only one dimension–the ant can only walk forward or back. But when viewed up close, one can see that the ant can actually move in another previously unseen direction–*in a circle around the power line*. An on-line article entitled **String Theory and M-Theory** by Markus Basan and Claus Basan describes how these dimensions work:

> "In M-theory on every point in four dimensional space-time there is a tiny curled up Calabi-Yau space of seven dimensions. All dimensions are closed . . . After the Big Bang only 4 dimensions expanded while the other 7 remained curled up. They are so small that they are impossible for us to see or detect. The strings vibrate in this 7D bundle . . . To produce new Calabi-Yau spaces, space can tear and repair itself after curving in another way. One can prove that the new shapes cannot be created without the tearing."

Dogon mythology provides similar details based on the drawing below of how a quantum string evolves in this 7D space:

Development Inside The Seed

> "The development of life inside the seed is represented by a series of figures called "drawings of the multiplication of the word of the *po*," which suggests the successive appearance of seven vibrations

developing in star-shaped fashion around a central
nucleus . . . the . . . figures show the development
of the vibrations in segments of increasing size, end-
ing with the seventh (at left) . . . their extremities
are at progressively greater distance from the center.
As a result, these extremities are on a spiral comparable to that of the *yala* of the *po*. The development
of the seed can take place only on the outside after
the seventh segment had gone thorough the "wall"
of the egg; because of this, it split up to form an
eighth element . . . In this way, the eight articulation
of the "word" within the seed will also have the
privilege of being the germ of the first in a new being." (*The Pale Fox* p. 137-138)

Details relating to the Dogon quantum thread bring the
mythological portrait of matter to completion. The narrative
of the Dogon creation story starts with Amma's egg, represented as a black hole, and takes us through each stage of
matter all the way down to massless particles or quantum
strings. But Brian Greene reminds us that, implicit within
string theory itself, is an intimate link between black holes
and massless particles that is best described by our mythological triad of gods, the three states of water:

"The connection between black holes and elementary particles . . . is closely akin to something we are
all familiar with from day-to-day life, known technically as phase transition. A simple example of a phase
transition is the one we mentioned . . . : water can
exist as a solid (ice), as a liquid (liquid water), and a
gas (steam). These are known as the *phases* of water, and the transformation from one form to another
is called a *phase transition* . . . Again, just as someone who has never before encountered liquid water
or solid ice would not immediately recognize that

they are two phases of the same underlying substance, physicists had not realized [before string
theory] that the kinds of black holes we were studying and elementary particles are actually two phases
of the same underlying stringy material." (*The Elegant Universe* p.332)

In essence, Dogon mythology seems to describe the
true underlying structure of matter, organizes it in the right
sequence, diagrams it correctly, and assigns the correct attributes to each of its components. Moreover, it does so
within the explicit context of a discussion of the structure of
matter. One of the underlying principles of science–called
Occam's razor–states that, all other considerations being
equal, we should prefer the simplest answer to any given
scientific problem. In this case, hard though it may be to
conceive, the simplest answer might well be that the Dogon
symbols in fact describe the components of matter they so
strongly resemble. Given the close and consistent correlation between Dogon descriptions, symbols and drawings
and those of science, any alternative suggestion of mere
coincidence would seem somehow to strain the very definition of the word *coincidence.*

Chapter 7: Egyptian Mythology

The many persistent similarities between Dogon and Egyptian religious symbols and lifestyles lead to a natural suggestion that modern Dogon society could actually represent a kind of modern remnant of ancient Egyptian culture. Up to this point in our discussion, we have mentioned several superficial points of commonality between the two societies which tend to support this idea. However, if Dogon stories and symbols are to be truly understood as surviving artifacts of such an exceedingly ancient tradition, then we ought to be able to equate many of the most essential Dogon concepts and symbols with specific counterparts in the Egyptian religion. Perhaps the most direct method for accomplishing this is to review similar elements of the Egyptian religion in the same context and sequence as they are presented by the storylines of the Dogon creation myth.

The surface storyline of the Egyptian religion begins with the god *Amen*, a likely equivalent to the Dogon god *Amma* both in name, attributes and actions. Unlike the Dogon religion, Egyptian mythology often produced a wealth of alternate names for any given god or goddess. For the most part, these aliases have been interpreted by modern scholars as expressions of various aspects of each god. Over the tens of centuries of Egyptian history many alternate names evolved for the god *Amen* including *Atum*, head of the Egyptian pantheon of gods in dynastic times and heir to *Amen's* attributes and icons. Many of the alternate names for *Amen* take the form of homonyms, anagrams and shortened or expanded versions of the name *Amen*. Godfrey Higgins, a nineteenth century writer and Hebrew scholar with no apparent knowledge of the Dogon religion, notes in his 1833 work **Anacalypsis** that if the letters of the Hebrew word *Omun*–a homonym for *Amen*–are reversed, the resulting word is *Numo*. Perhaps the earliest incarnation of *Amen*, which predates even the onset of writing in Egypt, is the god *Min*, whose icon is described as a meteoric stone not unlike the carved Dogon stone that represents *Amma's egg*. Another equivalent name for *Amen* is held by the lesser-known Egyptian god *Nemmhu*, whose name is a close phonetic match both for the Dogon *Nummo* and for the Sumerian mother goddess *Nammu*. Another more prominent Egyptian pseudonym for *Amen* is the Egyptian god *Menu*–again a recognizable phonetic anagram of *Nemmhu* and also the name of an important god in the ancient traditions of India. *Menu* has additional importance for this study because his hieroglyphic name consists of characters which represent the key symbols of the Dogon creation story: Water, a spiraling coil, a clay pot, the sun, and a drawing board:

The Egyptian tendency to use *words that sound alike* as a way to associate the true meanings of religious concepts is explained with great clarity by Serge Sauneron in his book **The Priests of Ancient Egypt:**

> "The Egyptians never considered their language–
> that corresponding to the hieroglyphs–as a *social* tool;
> for them, it always remained a resonant echo of the
> vital energy that had brought the universe to life, a

cosmic force. Thus, study of this language enabled them to "explain" the cosmos. It was word-play that served as the means of making these explanations.

The moment one understands that words are intimately linked to the essences of the beings or objects they indicate, resemblances between words cannot be fortuitous; they express a natural relationship, a subtle connection that priestly erudition would have to define . . .

This practice can seem childish and anything but serious. Yet its logic emerges if we try to understand the value the Egyptians placed on the pronunciation of words. Any superficial resemblance between two words was understood as conveying a direct connection between the two entities invoked. It thus became a general practice, employed in all periods and in all areas of inquiry, and in priestly lore it was the basic technique for explaining proper nouns, essentially the very means of defining the nature of the deities. This was the case with Amun, the great patron of Thebes. We do not know just what his name meant, but it was pronounced like another word meaning "to be hidden", and the scribes played on this resemblance to define Amun as the great god who hid his real appearance from his children . . . The mere similarity of the sounds of the two words was enough to arouse a suspicion on the part of the priests that there was some close relationship between them, and to find in it an explanation of the god's name: 'thus addressing the primordial god . . . as an invisible and hidden being, they invite him and exhort him, calling him Amun, to show and reveal himself.'" (*The Priests of Ancient Egypt* p. 125-127)

Some researchers interpret Egyptian wordplay as a fondness for puns, and suggest that the priests deliberately used them to disguise references to the innermost secrets of the Egyptian religion. In **The Sirius Mystery**, Robert K.G. Temple provides examples of what he sees as Egyptian puns and some of the difficulties they present to translators and researchers:

> "It should be noted that in Egyptian the hieroglyph *tchet* of a serpent means both 'serpent' and 'body'. The cobra hieroglyph *ara* means both 'serpent' and 'goddess'. Elsewhere we encounter *ara* frequently having the common general meaning of 'goddess'. The frequent incorporation of the serpent into late Sirius-lore among the Greeks probably stems from a pun or corruption of the Egyptian determinative form for 'goddess' . . . in fact, if an Egyptian were to write 'the Goddess Sirius' in hieroglyphs, the result . . . [could] also (by pun) be read quite literally as 'serpent's tooth' . . . In short, when does a pun cease to be a pun and merely consist of a mistranslation based on ignorance of the true subject-matter?" (*The Sirius Mystery* p. 175)

But to define these priestly "second meanings" as puns may not entirely do justice to the way in which they were used. Like the Egyptians, the Dogon also assign double meanings to words and phrases that are important to their religion. As an illustrative example, consider again the name of the Dogon creation story, *aduno so tanie*, which can mean "astonishing myth of the universe" or "secret symbols". Either phrase alone makes a correct statement about the Dogon creation story, but both statements together provide a much more exact definition of the creation story and how it works. This technique of using multiple meanings serves both to disguise the full import of a concept from the uninitiated, while at the same time enhancing a broader definition for the initiated.

There is a tradition among ancient mythologies that if

you were to learn the true name of a god, you would acquire power over that god. But given the way the Egyptian and Dogon languages work, one is led to suspect that this tradition has more to do with *secret meanings* than with actual *secret names*. The Egyptian phrase *bu maa*, which is translated as "truth", actually implies something that is a "longstanding perception", or something that has been "thoroughly examined". The Egyptian word *maa* means "to perceive or examine"–therefore *Maat* would literally mean "that which has been perceived or examined". The Egyptian word *bu* is used as a name for *Amen*–the timeless and infinite god. The **Dictionaire Dogon** tells us that the Dogon word *bu* means "timeless, endless or infinite". Consequently, a "thoroughly examined word or phrase" is one for which all of the multiple meanings are known, thereby providing true knowledge of–and power over–the concept it represents.

Egyptian mythology also presents us with recognizable counterparts to the perfect twin pair of the Dogon, the *Nummo*. The *male Nummo* is easily identified as the ram-headed Egyptian god *Khnoum*, closely associated with the Egyptian potter god *Ptah* and the later blacksmith god of Greek mythology *Hephaistos*. In Egyptian hieroglyphs, the name of the god *Khnoum* is rendered by one of the central Dogon symbols, the image of a simple clay pot:

In Egyptian mythology, *Khnoum* was credited with having created humankind from clay on his potter's wheel. His symbol was a ram with horizontally twisting horns–the variety of ram's horn that Ogotemmeli said was symbolically the older of the two types. Two existing Egyptian hymns identify *Khnoum* with at least ten other named deities, and H.W.F Saggs suggests in **Civilization Before Greek and Rome** that such identities could extend even outside of the Egyptian religion. *Khnoum*'s cult center in Egypt was called

Hermopolis by the Greeks; its Egyptian name was Khemenu which means "the Eight".

In the tradition of Heliopolis, the emergence of the first eight primeval gods and goddesses in male/female pairs seems to be in obvious agreement with the surface storyline events of the Dogon creation story. The eight ancestors of the Dogon resemble the four pairs of gods in the Egyptian Ennead–Geb and Nut, Shu and Tefnut, Isis and Osiris, Seth and Nephthys. Egyptian sources are not consistent in the symbolism they assign to these eight gods, but modern sources seem to agree that the first four are meant to represent the classic cosmic forces–*earth, water, wind and fire*. According to George Hart's **Dictionary of Egyptian Gods and Goddesses**, Geb was the earth god, Nut represented the sky, Shu represented sunlight and air, and Tefnut was a goddess of moisture. But based on linguistic similarities to other Egyptian hieroglyphic words, the name *Nut* seems most obviously related to other "Nu" words like *Nun*, which typically refer to water. The name *Tefnut* bears a similarity to Egyptian words beginning with "Te", such as *Tep* which means "fire" and *Teh* which means "flame". Even among mainstream archeologists, *Tefnut's* link to water is considered a rather weak one. George Hart writes in **A Dictionary of Egyptian Gods and Goddesses**:

> "Her connection with moisture is tenuously established from her position among deities representing cosmic elements and hints in inscriptions such as in the passage from the Pyramid Texts where the goddess creates pure water for the king's feet . . ." (*A Dictionary of Egyptian Gods and Goddesses* p. 213)

One possible reason for this confusion in meanings might be found in two separate passages from Dogon mythology. The first reference appears during a discussion of events surrounding the unformed universe, *Amma's egg*, prior to the "opening of Amma's eyes"–*the Big Bang*–in which the symbol of *earth* is counterposed with the symbol of *sky*. An equivalent scientific episode is described in the Big Bang theory, at a point in the cooling process of the universe. Lawrence M. Krauss writes in **Atom: An Odyssey from the Big Bang to Life on Earth . . . and Beyond**:

> "After 300,000 years, the temperature of the uni-
> verse evolved to close to the boiling point of iron. It
> now glowed uniformly white- hot . . . with every point
> glowing as bright as the sun. But there were not yet
> any vantage points from which to observe the sky.
> All there was was sky!" (*Atom* p. 72)

The second reference is found during the previously-quoted discussion of the structure of matter, in which the four categories of quantum particles are assigned the symbolism of *earth, water, fire and wind*. In all likelihood, the confusion in the Egyptian symbols is the result of a blending over time of these two separate references, leaving us with symbols for *earth, sky, air and water* instead of the expected *earth, water, wind and fire*. Furthermore, we have already linked the Dogon symbol of *fire* to particles of matter, and specifically to the symbol of the *electron*, which is a particle strongly affected by the electromagnetic force, which is in turn represented by the symbol for *water*. Because of the way in which these symbols relate to each other, it is easy to see how a confusion between the symbolic references for *fire* and *water* might occur.

From a modern perspective, the belief systems of Heliopolis and Hermopolis may seem like separate theologies, but Stephen Quirke expresses the opinion in his book **Ancient Egyptian Religion** that based on the surviving Egyptian texts, the more likely case is that the symbolism of both cults originated as a single set dating from the earliest days of the Egyptian religion, and that over time each cult center came to emphasize different aspects of the same original tradition.

Many of the signature attributes of the *female Nummo* of the Dogon are apparent in the Egyptian mother goddess *Neith*, described by most sources as the earliest Egyptian deity and as the mother of the numberless Egyptian gods. She was sometimes called the first birthgiver–the mother who gave birth to the sun at the beginning of existence. In images she is usually shown wearing the crown of Lower Egypt, and holding in her two hands a scepter and the *ankh*, the Egyptian sign of life. Perhaps originally a Libyan goddess, *Neith's* primary center of worship in Egypt was Sais, a city located in the Nile delta. In **A History of Ancient Egypt**, Nicholas Grimal tells of a temple founded by the first king of Egypt, Aha, and dedicated to *Neith* in honor of his wife Neithhotep, whose name in the Egyptian language meant "may Neith be appeased". Inscribed on a wall of this temple were the words, "I am all that was, that is, or that will be". The Greek philosopher Plato identified *Neith* with the Greek goddess *Athena*, the patron goddess of Athens. *Neith*, like the *female Nummo*, was a goddess of weaving, and was said by Egyptian mythology to have woven the world with her shuttle. Like the *female Nummo* of the Dogon, *Athena's* sacred animal was the serpent, and Greek mythology credited her with having taught the skills of agriculture to mankind. A later Greek myth in which *Athena* is portrayed giving dragon's teeth to Cadmus and Aeetes is closely linked to a similar Dogon story.

The first pivotal event in the surface storyline of the Egyptian religion centers around the emergence of the god *Amen/Atum* from the primeval waters of *Nun* on a mound of land called *the primeval hill*. In **A History of Ancient Egypt**, Nicholas Grimal provides a careful description of this event which calls to mind parallel aspects of the surface storyline of the Dogon:

"There are three Egyptian cosmologies, but they all represent political variations on a single theme: the sun's creation of the universe from a liquid element . . . The main system of cosmology was developed at Heliopolis, now a suburb of Cairo but once the ancient holy city where the pharaohs came to have their power consecrated. Not only was the Heliopolitan cosmology the earliest, but it also provided inspiration for Egyptian theologians throughout later periods of history.
The Heliopolitan cosmology described creation according to a scheme which is generally echoed by the other cosmologies. In the beginning was Nun, the uncontrolled liquid element, often translated as "chaos". Not a negative element in itself, Nun was simply an uncreated mass, without structure but containing within it the potential seeds of life."

"It was from this chaos that the sun emerged. The origin of the sun itself was not known, for it was said to have 'come into being out of itself'. It appeared on a mound of earth covered in pure sand emerging from water, taking the form of a standing stone, the *benben*. This *benben* stone was the focus of a cult in the temple at Heliopolis, which was considered to be the original site of creation . . . (*A History of Ancient Egypt* p. 41-42)"

Among later texts of the ancient religions of the world we can find many references that equate the first self-created god, in various forms and names, to *the sun*. But C. Staniland Wake–another nineteenth century writer–tells us in his article **The Origin of Serpent Worship** that prior to the existence of this solar identity, these same gods were closely linked with the star Sirius in its aspect as the herald of the sun at the start of the planting season. This observation by Wake is in complete agreement with the Dogon.

The *primeval hill,* which the *benben stone* was said to represent, was originally conceived of as a kind of mound in a shape similar to *Amma's egg,* and soon took on the form of a platform with stairs on each side, very much like the Dogon *granary.* In fact, *the primeval hill* was commonly represented by the Egyptian hieroglyph:

R.T. Rundle Clark says in **Myth and Symbol of Ancient Egypt** that the primeval hill is the concept that the step pyramid is meant to represent. We may recall that in Dogon mythology, the *granary* was an improved form of the simple mud huts of the Dogon, which took their shape after the pattern of the *anthill.* Clark suggests that the pyramid was the next logical step in a similar developmental progression in ancient Egypt. H.W.E. Saggs carries this thought a step further in a discussion of the *primeval mound* in **Civilization Before Greece and Rome:**

> "The mound of sand over a grave came to be thought of as magically equated with this primeval hill . . . What Imhotep did was to transform the old mound of sand, encased in a stepped arrangement of bricks, into a massive structure which covered and enclosed the complete tomb. The pyramid was therefore to the Egyptians, a representation, or commemoration, of the primeval hill. This explanation does not depend upon theoretical deduction: the connection between the pyramid and the god Atum on the primeval hill is explicitly made in a text carved on a pyramid; by this identification the pyramid was linked to the origins and maintenance of all life . . ." (*Civilization Before Greece and Rome* (p. 51).

The *benben* stone–shaped like *Amma's egg*–held a place

of importance and reverence in the ancient Egyptian religious traditions of Heliopolis that is comparable to *Amma's egg* in the Dogon religion. In the Egyptian mythology, *Ben* is another alternate name for the self-created god *Amen*. Like the icon of the god *Min*, the *benben stone* is described as a meteoric stone which was said to have been displayed in a place of public prominence at the top of a pillar or column of stone. The combination of the pillar and the *benben stone* came to be known as *the obelisk*, a fact which makes the relationship between the Egyptian gods *Ben* and *Menu* even more evident since an alternate form of the hieroglyphic word *menu* means *obelisk*. The *mastaba*, an oblong burial structure with slanted sides, is understood to have been an intermediate step between *the primeval mound* or *benben stone* and *the pyramid*. Nicholas Grimal writes:

> "The *mastaba* reproduced, within the home of the dead, the primeval mound from which Atum created the world–and so stood as a symbol of creation. The texts also suggest [that] Imhotep decided to turn the *mastaba* into a square and to cover it with a pyramid . . . . The step pyramid method of ascension was, however, superseded after just over a century by the smooth-sided pyramid of the Fourth Dynasty . . .
> The change to the smooth-sided pyramid and then the introduction of the *benben* [pointed capping] stone were intended to reconcile the conflict between Atum and Ra." (*A History of Ancient Egypt* p.126)

The conflict to which Grimal refers which brought about the transformation from flat-topped pyramids to the familiar peaked pyramid calls to mind the previously noted discrepancy in the dimensions of the Dogon granary. One can easily imagine a theological dispute between those who felt compelled to follow the creation story *description* of a flat-topped pyramid and those who were devoted to the creation story *mathematics*, which described a peaked pyramid. The suggestion is that Imhotep resolved an impasse by adding the symbol of an unimpeachable religious icon, *the benben stone*, to the top of the step-pyramid–a move that would be comparable to adding a cross to the top of a church–and in the end satisfied both factions. Given what we know from the Dogon creation story about the mathematics of the granary, it is also completely understandable that the largest surviving step-pyramid, built by King Zoser and located at Saqqara, consisted of six steps leading to a flat platform, because if we follow the creation story dimensions for the granary and make the choice to incorporate the steps into the face of each side of a flat-topped platform, the mathematics of the structure automatically work out to six steps.

From a linguistic standpoint there are clear connections between the Egyptian pyramid and the Dogon concept of the granary. The Egyptian hieroglyphic word for *granary* or warehouse is *ukher*, and the base of a pyramid is called *ukha theb-t*. As we recall from our previous summary of the Dogon creation story, the fire of the first smithy was established on the flat platform at the top of the granary. We also know that in some ancient cultures flat-topped pyramids were used as altars of sacrifice. So it comes as no surprise that the Egyptian word *ukha* means *fire altar*. There is also ample linguistic evidence to associate the word *benben* with *Amma's egg* of the Dogon. There is an alternate form of the word *benben* which means "to hasten", and which defines the Dogon sense of *Amma's* efforts to "begin in a dynamic sense" the processes of the universe. This interpretation is wholly reinforced when we look to the word in the Egyptian language for "to begin", which is *shaa*, since Wallis Budge lists a second word with the same pronunciation which means "granary". Moreover, the dual symbolism of *benben* as both *Amma's egg* and *the granary* is again supported when we look to the Egyptian word *sehu*, which means "to collect, to gather" and "gathered into the store", and a second word clearly related to it, *sehu-t*, which means "egg".

This relationship between the *benben stone* and *Amma's egg* makes it much easier to understand the otherwise obscure Egyptian symbol of the *scarab*. In Egyptian mythology, the *scarab* is known to represent the dung beetle, an insect which lays its eggs rolled up inside a ball of dung. This ball is an obvious natural counterpart to *Amma's egg*, which in similar fashion contained the coiled-up seeds of the unformed universe. Based on this identity, it is relatively easy to see how the dung beetle or *scarab* might have come to represent the creative force behind the egg.

After *Amma's egg*–the Dogon equivalent of the unformed universe–the first component in our discussion of the structure of matter was the atom-like *po*. If we search through Sir Wallis Budge's hieroglyphic dictionary for words similar to *po*, we find an entry for the name of an Egyptian god *Pau*–a homonym for the Dogon word *po*. According to Budge, *Pau* may mean "he who is; he who exists; the self-existent". We can relate this word more specifically to the concept of an atom by looking to the related Egyptian word *pau-t*, which means "matter" or "substance". As mentioned earlier, the Dogon tell us that *po* comes from the same root as *polo*, which means "beginning", so it is not surprising that for the Egyptians, *pau* also means "primeval time", and *pauti taui* means "the beginning of time".

As we recall, the Dogon tell us that the *sene seed*–the apparent equivalent of *electrons, protons and neutrons*–comingled at the center of the *po*, just as protons and neutrons comingle to form the *nucleus* of an atom. Stephen Hawking tells us in **A Brief History of Time** that *protons and neutrons* consist of known combinations of *quarks*:

> "A proton or a neutron is made up of three quarks . . .
> a proton contains two up quarks and one down quark;

a neutron contains two down quarks and one up. We can create particles made up of other quarks . . . but these all have a much greater mass and decay very rapidly into protons and neutrons." (*A Brief History of Time* p. 65)

So if we were looking for a sensible hieroglyph to represent either a *proton or a neutron*, we would expect it to somehow convey to us the idea of a *particle* created by the binding of *three components*. Furthermore, we would expect the Egyptian word to be linguistically related to the Dogon word *sene*. Using these criteria as a basis for a search of the hieroglyphic dictionary, we easily find the word *sen*, meaning "they, them, their", and represented as:

—o—

Ŏ |||

An alternate reading of this hieroglyph might be, "a particle [clay pot] is created by the binding [knotted rope] of three elements [the number three]." The same Dogon word *sene* seems also to refer to an *electron*, described as surrounding the *po* and making it visible by "crossing" in all directions to form a *nest*, just as actual electrons circle the nucleus of an atom. Again, if we were to imagine an ideal configuration of hieroglyphs for this word, we would expect it to include a reference to the *electromagnetic force* and to an *electron orbit*. In Egyptian hieroglyphs, the likely equivalent word for *nest* is *aunnu*, whose presumed root word is *aun*, which means "to open" . Among the hieroglyphic characters that comprise the word *aun*, we find a most recognizable Egyptian counterpart to the Dogon diagram of an *electron orbit* joined with the symbol for water– the icon we previously associated with *the electromagnetic force*. An alternate reading of this hieroglyph might be, "That which orbits due to the electromagnetic force."

~~~~~~~~

We may recall that it was the *sene seed* as *an electron* which played the role of the 1/2 spin particle in the Dogon story of the *stolen fire of the Nummo*. We suggested that the word *stolen* was a reference to the binding of two atoms via a shared electron to form a molecule. Based on this reading, we can interpret further connections between the Dogon word *sene* and the Egyptian word *sen*, which has two appropriate alternate meanings—one of which is "to bind", and the other is "thief"—a meaning which clearly recalls the Dogon exclamation of "stolen".

The next aspect of Dogon symbols relating to atomic structure involve the Dogon creative mindset of *bummo, yala, tonu and toy*. We previously related the phases of this creative process to the four quantum forces—*the gravitational force, the electromagnetic force, the strong nuclear force and the weak nuclear force*. In **Legends of the Egyptian Gods**, E.A.Wallis Budge provides an Egyptian example of this same mindset when he relates the legend of the creation of the universe by the god *Khepera*. He writes:

> "The story of the Creation is supposed to be told by the god Neb-er-tcher . . . This name means the "Lord to the uttermost limit," and the character of the god suggests that the word "limit" refers to time and space, and that he was, in fact, the Everlasting God of the Universe . . . Where and how Neb-er-tcher existed is not said, but it seems as if he was believed to have been an almighty and invisible power which

filled all space. It seems also that a desire arose in him to create the world, and in order to do this he took upon himself the form of the god Khepera . . . When this transformation . . . took place the heavens and the earth had not been created, but there seems to have existed a vast mass of water, or world-ocean, called Nu . . . and it must have been in this that the transformation took place. In this celestial ocean were the germs of all the living things which afterwards took form in heaven and on earth, but they existed in a state of inertness and helplessness . . . Khepera gave being to himself by uttering his own name . . . and he made use of words in providing himself with a place on which to stand . . . [one] version [of the creation story] speaks of a heart-soul as assisting Khepera in his first creative acts; and we may assume that he thought out in his heart what manner of thing he wished to create, then by uttering its name caused his thought to take concrete form. This process of thinking out the existence of things is expressed in Egyptian by the words which mean "laying the foundation in the heart."

In arranging his thoughts and their visible forms Khepera was assisted by the goddess Maat, who is usually regarded as the goddess of law, order, and truth . . . In this legend, however, she seems to play the part of Wisdom . . . for it was by Maat that he "laid the foundation." (*Legends of the Egyptian Gods* p. xvii)

This Egyptian concept of "laying a foundation", which appears in the context of a myth that describes the creation of the matter of the universe, closely resembles the Dogon creative process of *bummo, yala, tonu and toy,* and is explained by means of the same architectural metaphor that is used by Dogon mythology. There are also linguistic links between Egyptian words and the Dogon concepts represented by *bummo, yala, tonu and toy*. When we examine these associations, it is important to remember that in the Egyptian hieroglyphic language, just as in ancient Hebrew, the vowel sounds were only implied, and might well be as accurately represented by other vowel sounds. The hieroglyphic counterpart of the Dogon word *bummo*, which most closely represents the conceptual stage of a creative act, is *bu maa*, which means "truth" and is a synonym for *Maat* and is based on the same root word *maa*. The Egyptian word *maa* actually means "to examine" or "to perceive", a meaning which makes it a fair representation of the conceptual stage of an idea or project. The Dogon word *yala* is defined by the laying of stones to define the outline of a structure. Its hieroglyphic counterpart is *ahau*, which means "delimitation posts" or "boundaries". The third Dogon stage of *tonu* is defined as an approximation of the object to be created. Its Egyptian counterpart is *teni*, which means "to estimate". The final Dogon creational stage is called *toy or toymu*, and is thought of as the finishing step of an object. The corresponding hieroglyphic word is *temau*, which means "complete", the same concept which is reflected in the name of the Egyptian god *Atum or Tum*, whose name, according to Robert Graves' **New Larousse Encyclopedia of Mythology**, comes from a root which means "to be complete".

The phrase "laying a foundation in the heart" itself is expressed in the hieroglyphic language by the phrase *senti ta*. One meaning of the word *sen* is "to create", and the word *senti* ("foundation") means "to found" or "to establish". There is also a homonym for the word *ta* which means "time". So the spoken phrase *senti ta* could just as easily be used to express the phrase "to create or establish time"– from a scientific standpoint, a perfectly appropriate act for a self-created god.

For the Dogon, the most fundamental component of the

structure of matter was the *thread* woven by the *spider of the sene*, whose name was *Dada*. If we were to pursue the word *dada* in the Egyptian hieroglyphic language, we might first disregard what for the Egyptians would be the two implied "*a*" vowel sounds, and focus instead on the consonants "*dd*". Dr. Ramses Seleem tells us in his recent translation of the **Egyptian Book of the Dead**:

> "The Egyptian words for "language" are *Ddt, Medu,* or *Ra-N-Kemit.* The root of the word *Ddt* is the verb *Dd,* which means "to say", "speak", or "declare". The utterance of sound is energy resonating in a spiral form, which is represented by the snake, the symbol of primordial energy . . ." (*The Illustrated Egyptian Book of the Dead* p. 35)

The previous passage from Budge tells us that *speech*– the very symbol of the spiraling primordial energy–is precisely the tool by which the Egyptian god *Khepera* created the universe. So by this correspondence, the Egyptian creative impulse and formative power of the universe equates conceptually and linguistically to the spiraling thread woven by the Dogon spider *Dada*.

All of this brings us back to *Neith*, the primeval goddess who was distinct from *Amen* and held no specific position in the surface story of the Egyptians, but yet was still considered to be the mother of all of the other Egyptian gods and goddesses, and who for some reason had no obvious counterpart in the Dogon religion. Based on previous discussion, we recall that central symbols of Dogon mythology can be shown to represent each of the scientific building blocks of matter, starting with the *atom*, working down to *electrons, protons and neutrons*, continuing on to *quantum particles and quantum forces*, and culminating in the *quantum string*. The Dogon equate the four categories of quantum particles with the symbols "earth, water, fire and wind", and refer to the bottom-most component–*the quantum string*– as a *thread*. For both the Dogon religion and modern science, all matter is a by-product of the movement or vibration of *quantum threads*. When we look to Egyptian hieroglyphs, we find that the word for "thread" is *ntt-t* and the word for "weaving" is *ntt*–both from the same root as the word *Net* which is the Egyptian name for *Neith*. What this implies is that the true counterpart of *Neith* might well be the Dogon spider *Dada*, the weaver of the quantum thread. In fact, the connection between the Dogon spider and the Egyptian mother goddess is strengthened by an entry in the **Dictionnaire Dogon**. According to this dictionary, the Dogon word *dada* means "mother".

When Egyptian mythology states that *Neith* "wove the world on her shuttle", it is significant that it essentially attributes the existence of the world to the movement of threads–just like Dogon mythology and modern string theory. Moreover, the hieroglyphic language provides us with a direct connection to the coiled quantum thread of the Dogon by means of an alternate hieroglyphic word for "thread", *thes-t*, which comes from the root word *thes*, which carries two meanings: "to coil" and "to weave".

Based on previous discussion, if the Egyptian word *ntt*, which means "to weave, to bind, to tie", were indeed to represent the scientific concept of the *quantum string*, then we would expect the hieroglyphic characters which comprise the word to reflect some recognizable feature relating to the weaving of quantum strings. In their book **The Matter Myth**, Paul Davies and John Gribben present a series of diagrams which represent two types of intersection of quantum strings.

Quantum String Intersections

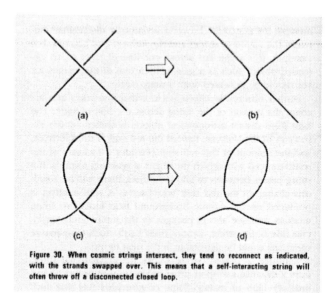

Figure 30. When cosmic strings intersect, they tend to reconnect as indicated, with the strands swapped over. This means that a self-interacting string will often throw off a disconnected closed loop.

The Egyptian hieroglyphic word *ntt* is written in a variety of ways. Two of the more common forms include as dominant characters symbols which *precisely* match the above diagrams, and thereby reflect a relationship to the weaving of quantum strings.

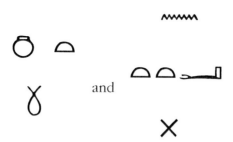

The Egyptian name for the goddess *Neith* is *Net*, and can be written hieroglyphically in many different forms. We can only presume that if *Neith* in one of her aspects was meant to represent a *quantum string*, then the hieroglyphic name of *Neith* would in some way reflect that scientific meaning. Compare the hieroglyph below for *Neith* with a corresponding diagram beneath it from Brian Greene's **The Elegant Universe**, which illustrates a more complex interaction of quantum strings:

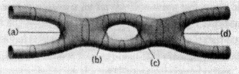

Complex Interaction of Quantum String

Figure 12.4 The quantum frenzy can cause a string/antistring pair to erupt (b) and annihilate (c), yielding a more complicated interaction.

We know that the first emergent gods of the Heliopolitan tradition were *Geb, Nut, Shu and Tefnut*–the same gods we previously associated with *earth, water, wind and fire*. With *Neith* as the mother goddess, we therefore have at the very foundation of the Egyptian religion the unmistakable symbol for a *quantum thread* producing the four categories of *quantum particles*, expressed in virtually the same terms as the Dogon. So the sense in which *Neith* can be considered the mother of all the gods is the same sense in which the *quantum string* can be considered the source of all matter. In support of this interpretation of the goddess *Neith* as a *quantum string*, we find the following statement in an article by Katherine Griffis-Greenberg, entitled **Neith: Goddess of the Beginning, the Beyond, and the End**:

"Causing matter to exist and to live is the primary nature in Neith's primeval role in creation. That she does so without assistance of other deities is attested to her from the Pyramid Texts to the end of ancient Egyptian culture. Of all Egyptian gods and goddesses, Neith is often referred to in Egyptian texts as the "eldest", and even as the "first" deity. She is reputed, especially in the Late Period, to be the great creator of the world, and is often called by some scholars the equivalent of the creator gods such as Atum and Ptah.

As in the case of these primeval gods (though generally referred to as male), Neith is described in texts as either undifferentiated in gender or possessing both genders. As such, Neith should not be seen as a "original mother goddess" figure, as indicated in some references, but as an androgynous deity who creates the world from self-generation. However, unlike these gods who act after "emerging" from the void, the texts from all periods of Egyptian history indicate that she is, in fact, representation of the first conscious Act of Creation from the Void, who takes the inert potential of Nun and cause creation to begin."
(*Neith: Goddess of the Beginning, the Beyond, and the End* p. 3)

So we see that by means of myths and hieroglyphs, the Egyptian religion has succeeded in presenting the clearest of definitions of quantum strings, their purpose and structure, and the most common ways they interact, using precise duplicates of not *one* but *three* highly recognizable scientific diagrams from string theory, all within the explicit context of a discussion of the structure of matter.

When Egyptian mythology speaks of *Neith*–our symbol for the *quantum string*–creating matter from the "inert potential of Nun", we quickly realize that the concept of *Nun* must also have some significance related to quantum and atomic science. So again we look for an obvious hieroglyph reference to define for us what aspect of science that might be. What we find, in Dogon mythological terms, are *particles and waves*, science's quintessential building blocks of matter.

If we explore the Egyptian hieroglyphic words for *thread* we are also led to significant confirmation of vibrating quantum strings. The first of these comes from the word *set*, meaning "thread, string, cord", which is written by the combination of glyphs below, and a related word *sett*, which means "to tremble". The association of these words also provides a clue as to why we find no entry in Budge's hieroglyphic dictionary for the phrase "to vibrate"–apparently Budge chose to interpret the many Egyptian references to vibrations with a phrase of very similar meaning, "to tremble".

The Egyptian hieroglyphic language also provides us with confirmation of M-theory, its discussion of Calabi-Yau spaces, and the tearing of curved space. This confirmation is found when we trace the Egyptian words for "spacious" *(pet)* and for "to tear" *(peth)*. It is interesting to note that the word *peth* bears a relationship to the name of the Egyptian god *Pteh (Ptah)*, who was defined by Wallis Budge as "the architect of heaven and earth". Compare the diagram from ***The Elegant Universe*** below, representing the tearing of a Calabi-Yau space, with the Egyptian hieroglyph for the word "to tear" below it.

The Tearing of Calabi-Yau Space

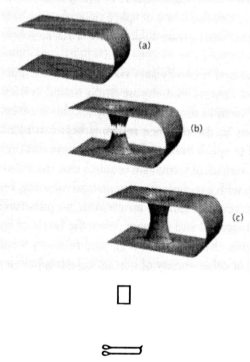

One of the ways in which the Egyptian hieroglyphic language expresses itself is by the use of determinatives–characters which are included among the glyphs of a word specifically to establish the context of the word. We find this same method at use among words that relate to scientific concepts. For instance the character of the hemisphere is commonly found in words relating to the structure of matter, and the character of the square seems to be evident in words relating to concepts of space/time. There is a clear logic to these choices. The figure of a square seems like the quintessential diagram to define a "space". Likewise, there is ample mythological precedent for the use of a hemisphere as a representation of the earth, and the earth as a metaphor for matter.

⌒ ▯

The identification of *Neith* and *the Ennead gods* of Egyptian mythology with components of atomic structure presents us with an intriguing possibility–that there might well have been an intentional symbolic relationship between the original gods of the Heliopolitan tradition and scientific concepts relating to the Big Bang and the creation of matter. When we examine these symbols from this perspective, and consider what we already have learned about the earliest Egyptian gods, a suggestive pattern begins to emerge. The gods *Ben and Min*–essentially two different names for the same god–are identified by the meteoric stone that in Dogon culture represents the unformed universe. *Amen,* the counterpart of the Dogon god *Amma,* represents the creative impulse by which the Big Bang was initiated–as the Dogon say, the very wind that scattered future matter to all corners of the universe. *Neith* represents the *quantum string*–the fundamental source of the vibrations of matter. *Geb, Nut, Shu and Tefnut* stand for the four categories of quantum particles, which the Dogon refer to symbolically as *earth, water, wind and fire.* The god *Menu* is a composite of the four quantum forces–in a sense virtually a formula for matter. Strong support for this interpretation is found in the symbols of his hieroglyphic name, which take on new meaning when we look at them from this scientific perspective:

SYMBOL	DOGON MEANING	SCIENTIFIC MEANING
℮	*Spider's thread*	*Quantum string*
☉	*Bummo (Earth/draw together)*	*Gravitational force (orbit)*
∿∿∿	*Yala (Water/bumpy)*	*Electromagnetic force*
◯	*Tonu (Fire/bows its head)*	*Weak nuclear force (particle)*
⌣	*Toy (Wind/drawing board or weaving loom*	*Strong nuclear force (draws the atom)*

This apparent correlation between the first Egyptian gods and aspects of quantum science presents us with what may be a valuable new tool for interpreting the symbols of the Egyptian religion. It implies that we might be able to segregate an "original" set of Egyptian gods and goddesses from later ones based on the degree to which the characters of their hieroglyphic names define the property of science they are understood to symbolize. Moreover, it provides a means for us to cross-check the validity of the scientific meanings we have proposed for Dogon symbols. Using this method, we are able to validate the scientific meanings of three key symbols by examining the hieroglyphic structure of the word *un*, which means "to be" or "to exist" (not surprisingly, *unun* also means "to tremble", and "to do work in a field"). The glyphs for *un* simply and appropriately consist of the symbol for the quantum string, the symbol for the electromagnetic force, and the symbol for an electron orbit:

One of the more difficult aspects of quantum theory relates to the seeming paradoxes that occur when we examine the behavior of matter at the most fundamental levels. Richard Feynmen says in **The Character of Physical Law** that the most important of these paradoxes can be demonstrated by a single experiment, conducted in three phases. Imagine that we have a barrier with an opening in the center, and a second barrier beyond it with two openings, each located a third of the way from either end. Beyond the second barrier we have placed a detector which is capable of recording anything that passes beyond the second barrier.

In the first phase of the experiment, we fire bullets in random directions through the opening of the first barrier. Some of these pass through the openings of the second barrier and are recorded by the detector. Because the bullets are fired one at a time, they do not interfere with each other, and so create a specific type of identifiable pattern on the detector.

In the second phase of the experiment, we send waves of water through the opening of the first barrier. Some of these pass through the openings in the second barrier, and the intensity of the waves is recorded by the detector. In this case, the waves do interfere with each other, just as the waves of a passing boat will interfere with a nearby water-skier. Some of the waves cancel each other out while other waves reinforce each other, and so create a different type of recognizable pattern on the detector.

Feynman says that when we try this same experiment using electrons instead of bullets, some unusual things happen. If we monitor the two openings in the second barrier and observe the electrons as they pass, they form a pattern on the detector that is similar to the one created by bullets. In other words, the electrons behave as particles. However, if we do *not* monitor the electrons, but simply record their arrival at the detector, they form a pattern that is similar to the one created by waves of water. What scientists infer from this is that electrons can behave like particles or like waves, and that the act of observation somehow causes the difference in behavior. The method used in most cases to observe electrons is to shine a very bright light on them, which might lead us to believe that the presence of light causes the difference. But in fact, the difference occurs regardless of the method used to detect the electrons. The more precise the method is at detecting the electrons, the more the pattern created is like that of particles.

This aspect of behavior of electrons seems to be absolutely fundamental to the nature of matter, so if the Egyptian and Dogon creation myths are to be considered true examples of informed science, then it would be hard to imagine that the subject would not be discussed somewhere in these mythologies. And since the subject is so very basic to the workings of matter, the most obvious place to look for it would be near the beginning of the process of creation. What quantum experiments describe is an underlying aspect of matter that behaves like waves of water, but is changed by mere perception into what we see as organized particles of matter.

If we consider the details of the Heliopolitan creation tradition of Egypt discussed previously, what we recall is the description of an unformed waterlike chaos called *Nun*. The god *Khepera*, with the aid of *Maat*–what Egyptologists interpret as Truth or Order–is able to speak a word (the Dogon say "weave a word") and thereby create physical aspects of the tangible world from the unrealized potential of *Nun*. We have previously talked about the Egyptian word *Maat* and its root word *maa* and suggested based on entries in the **Egyptian Hieroglyphic Dictionary** and the **Dictionaire Dogon** that a more accurate translation of *maa* might be "to examine or to perceive". The word *Khepera* comes from a root which means "to transform". Based on these definitions, what the Egyptian self-created god has actually done is take the unrealized waterlike potential of *Nun* and simply by perceiving it, transmuted it into the quantum threads that form the words of matter. Both the Egyptians and the Dogon call this a process of "laying a foundation", and in fact that is precisely what it is–the method by which the foundation of matter is laid.

To understand the phrase "laying a foundation in the heart", we need only explore the various Egyptian hieroglyphic words for "heart" and the words they sound like. One word for heart is *hat*, which can mean "the beginning" or "the frontier". In this context, we can see the process as that of laying a foundation at the beginning or at the frontier of matter. Another word for heart is *het*, which can also mean "the foremost part" or "the mind". In this context, the process might be equally well seen as one of laying a foundation for reality in the mind. An alternate meaning for *het* is "pot", our mythological symbol for a particle. So in this sense, we see the phrase as a reference to "laying a foundation for particles".

We can see that what Egyptian mythology has expressed in the clearest of terms is Feynman's paradox of matter– that somehow what we call "reality" acts as a kind of filter to present the underlying version of matter in an ordered way. Egyptian mythology confirms this interpretation by using the word *Maat*, one meaning of which is "order". The suggestion is that whenever this underlying reality goes unperceived, it behaves like waves; once it is perceived, it behaves like particles. This implies that what we call "reality" may actually be a translated or interpreted version of some other more fundamental existence.

Since Egyptian mythology seems to describe this process, it only makes sense to explore the hieroglyphic words relating to it and see what more we can learn. What we soon find is that there is an alternate word for "thread" which is *nu-t*, and which is written in hieroglyphs as:

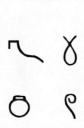

What the glyphs above show is the symbol of the *wavy line of water* and the cutting edge of an *adze*, which means to "select, choose or shape", followed by the symbols for a *particle*, a *quantum string* and the looped *quantum string intersection*. The *adze* is the tool often carried by *Amen* in Egyptian art. The scientific implication is that the act of observation somehow causes quantum threads to be shaved like planed wood. Likewise, we find many of these same glyphs in the Egyptian word for "to look, to observe":

The quantum interaction by which waves are transformed into particles seems to be a critical one in which the act of perception makes an unrealized potential "real", so it also makes sense to examine the Egyptian word for "real". When we search for this word in the hieroglyphic dictionary, what we find–appropriately and quite remarkably–is that the Egyptian word for "real" is *maa*.

The quantum paradox of waves and particles and their relationship to corresponding concepts in the Egyptian religion prepare us at last to understand the name of the Egyptian god *Amen*, known as "the hidden one", and the counterpart to the Dogon god *Amma*. The name includes the following three glyphs which we have not yet encountered in our study, whose meanings are taken from the **Hieroglyphic Dictionary**:

 meaning "place or sanctuary",

 meaning "to hide or to be hidden", and

meaning "to interfere".

The name of *Amen* is written:

A literal and most understandable reading of the name of *Amen* might be "That which draws or weaves waves into particles in a place hidden from interference."

Chapter 8: Genetics and Sexual Reproduction

The more we grow familiar with the Dogon creation story and its symbols, the more obvious it becomes that the correlations with fact extend beyond just the science of astrophysics. Indeed, one of the more remarkable aspects of the Dogon creation story is the way in which it seems to have incorporated three separate concurrent creational subplots into the context of a single mythological narrative. As mentioned previously, the first of these subplots tells the story of the Big Bang and the creation of matter–a theme that is altogether appropriate for a creation myth. The second subplot focuses on an equally appropriate creation topic–the story of genetics and sexual reproduction. We have already noticed obvious reproductive references during our discussion of the surface storyline of the Dogon. But even more remarkably, this second mythological subplot establishes itself by assigning an alternate set of meanings to the same basic symbols that define the concepts of atomic and quantum structure. And like the story of the Big Bang, this subplot begins with the same initiating symbol–*Amma's egg*. In **The Pale Fox**, Griaule and Dieterlen provide us with a description and a diagram of *Amma's egg* in its reproductive aspect.

> "Amma's egg is represented in the form of an oblong picture covered with signs, called "womb of all world signs", the center of which is the umbilicus . . . The oval contained the 266 "signs of Amma" (*amma bummo).*" (*The Pale Fox* p. 84)

Amma's Egg

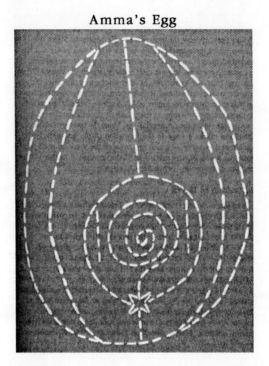

On this alternate symbolic level, *Amma's egg* represents a womb–the source of reproductive life–and at its
center is a spiral containing the 266 potential seeds or signs.
A spiral taken in the context of a womb can only call to
mind the spiraling helix of DNA, which science tells us
houses all of the seeds of potential that control reproductive
growth. Looking at *Amma's egg* and its related mythological symbols from this perspective, we can again find many
obvious Dogon and Egyptian references to support this alternate interpretation. The most obvious place to start is
with the *benben stone*–the Egyptian counterpart to *Amma's
egg*. Robert Bauval and Adrian Gilbert describe the *benben
stone* and what we know of its history in Egyptian culture in
The Orion Mystery:

> "At Heliopolis there was an important sacred hill or
> mound upon which the First Sunrise had taken place,

and belief has it that the sacred pillar stood on this holy mound prior to the Pyramid Age.

At the beginning of the Pyramid Age, another, even more sacred relic either replaced the sacred pillar or, more likely, was placed upon it. This was the Benben, a mysterious conical stone which . . . was credited with cosmic origins. The Benben Stone was housed in the Temple of the Phoenix and was symbolic of this legendary cosmic bird of regeneration, rebirth and calendric cycles. In Ancient Egyptian art the phoenix was usually depicted as a grey heron, perhaps because of the heron's migratory habits; it was believed that the phoenix came to Heliopolis to mark important cycles and the birth of a new age. Its first coming seems to have produced the cult of the Benben Stone, probably considered the divine 'seed' of the prodigal cosmic bird. This idea . . . is evident from the root word *ben* or *benben* which can mean human sperm, human ejaculation or the seeding of a womb. The mysterious Benben Stone disappeared long before Herodotus visited Egypt but not before it had bequeathed its name to the apex stone or pyramidion usually placed on top of pyramids and, later, the head of an obelisk." (*The Orion Mystery* p.17)

Like *Amma's egg*, Bauval and Gilbert describe the *benben* stone as a womb, and cite reproductive meanings as the root of the word *benben*. We recall that the dual symbolism of *Amma's egg* was previously established by the relationship of *Amma's egg* to the Dogon *granary*, and the Egyptian word *sehu*, which means "to collect, to gather" and "gathered into the store", and the related word *sehu-t*, which means "egg". In fact, throughout history the very term *egg* has often been used as a kind of defining metaphor for reproduction and rebirth. Dogon symbolism of *the granary* itself brings the idea of a womb directly into focus in another way, since its external structure was thought to represent a woman lying on her back, with the doorway symbolizing her sexual part. From this point of view, the interior of *the granary* is well positioned to symbolize a womb.

The Dogon tell us that the spiral at the center of the womb contains the 266 seeds of reproductive potential. If, as we said, the spiral reminds us of DNA, then the 266 seeds would naturally make us think of chromosomes and genes - the component building blocks of DNA. This suggests that if we want to understand these symbols, our best approach might be to review what we know about chromosomes.

Every human cell includes 23 pairs of chromosomes, one of which is responsible for establishing the sex of the individual. Modern science groups the first 22 pairs of chromosomes together and calls them *autosomes*, but it is the structure of the final pair of chromosomes that ultimately determines which sex the baby will be. These sex-determining chromosomes can be shaped either like an X with four branches, or like a Y with three branches, and so they are called the *X and Y chromosomes*. For a person to develop as a female, this 23rd chromosome pair must consist of two X chromosomes; for a person to be male, it must consist of an X and a Y chromosome. Consequently during sexual reproduction, one X chromosome from the mother matches up with either an X or a Y chromosome from the father and thereby produces a female or a male child.

When discussing the 23 pairs of chromosomes, modern genetics makes a distinction between the 22 autosomes and the final pair of sex-determining chromosomes, since this unique pair represents an exception to a rule that is worthy of separate discussion. Dogon mythology takes a similar approach when it organizes the 266 seeds or signs of *Amma's egg*. In **The Pale Fox**, Griaule and Dieterlen tell us about the organization of this spiral of signs within the womb.

"The sixty-six *yala* of the central spiral break down
as follows: twenty-two at the center for the *po*, then
forty for eight seeds, at the ratio of five per seed, and
finally four for the *scnc* at the tip of the spiral. The
po, in the body of which Amma will build the world,
is here understood to be the principle and prefigura-
tion of the seed . . . it has twenty-two *yala*.
At the center of the spiral of the twenty-two *yala* of
the *po*, first six *yala* are counted (as were the first six
bummo in the breakdown of the picture of the signs).
These six *yala* are the "sex of the po"; their number
connotes the initial masculinity of the *po's* sex, for
three will represent, in man, the penis and the two
testicles. The repetition of the number 3 underscores
another fundamental aspect of Amma's second genesis: twinness . . .
The six *yala* of the "sex of the *po*" are considered as
the *yala* of the "sex" of the universe; they will also
be the image of the sex of the first animate being
formed in Amma's womb, the *nommo anagonno*, symbol of the human fetus." (*The Pale Fox* p.121-122)

The Dogon description above compares favorably with
the modern scientific understanding of the 22 human autosomes and the final sex-determining chromosome. The parallel nature of these descriptions provide us with a new
basis for interpreting the Dogon numerological assignments
of 4 (female) and 3 (male), because these numbers correspond to the X and Y chromosomes of science–the first with
4 branches which produces a female fetus, the second with
3 branches which produces a male. Based on this interpretation, it is completely understandable that the number 7
would then be numerlogically assigned to *the individual*, since
it is the pairing of the X and the Y chromosomes that determines the sex of the individual. Traces of this same system of
numerology can be found in Egyptian heiroglyphs, where:

⊓ means "she", ⤳ means "he",

⤳ ⤳   ⊜

⤳ ⤳ means "four" and ⊓⤳ means "seven"

During prior discussions of atomic and quantum structure, we found that the tribal drawings of the Dogon worked to reinforce the similarities between mythological descriptions of Dogon symbols and those from science. As we look at these same symbols from the perspective of sexual reproduction and genetics, we find that this is again the case. The identification of Dogon symbols with the science of genetics can be affirmed almost beyond dispute when we compare a scientific diagram relating to *mitosis* with the Dogon drawing of the *yala* of the *egg of nommo anagonno*:

Chromosomes & Spindles During Mitosis

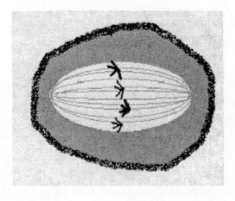

Yala of Egg of Nommo Anagonno

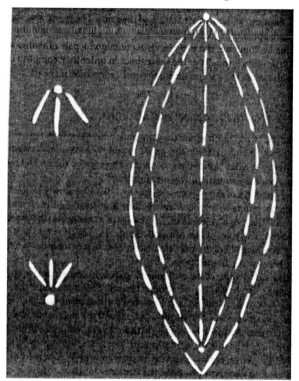

Each of the two above diagrams depicts a stage in the process of *mitosis*, or the simple asexual division of a cell, during which the chromosomes duplicate themselves, and spindles form which allow the chromosomes to move to opposite ends of the cell prior to splitting. In **The Pale Fox**, Griaule and Dieterlen describe the Dogon understanding of this same process in essentially scientific terms:

> " . . . during the division of the *yala*, the respective position of the *amma giru*, in relation to all those of the egg of the *nommo anagonno*, will play an essential role of orientation, as well as function as a sort of initial framework. Indeed, the *yala* of the four body *kikinu* placed themselves at the top of the egg (in

the form of three strokes emerging from a central point) dominating it somewhat like the ribs of an umbrella. At the opposite end, the *yala* of the sex *kikinu* became inverted, placing themselves in the same way at the bottom of the egg.

To emphasize the respective roles [the Dogon say]:

" . . . the *yala* of the egg of *nommo anagonno* is stretched like the world that is going to spread itself out . . . the *yala* of the *nommo (anagonno)* caused the elongation (enlargement, growth) of the world." In fact the formed being will be complete and alive, therefore pure, and a promoter of general fertility." (*The Pale Fox* p. 161-162)

In the Egyptian language, we find an image similar to these diagrams of chromosomes and spindles represented in the prominent hieroglyphic character of the word *mes en*–perhaps a form of the word *sen*–which means "born of, brought forth by", and which is the single hieroglyphic character used to write the word *mesi*, which means "to bear, to give birth to, to produce, to fashion" The same symbol is prominently seen in the word *messiu*, which means "those who are born, children", and *mes*, which means "to weave, to spin".

Looking further in the Egyptian language, we find another similar word *sen*, which means "to copy, to make a likeness of anything". An appropriate homonym or perhaps pun on the word *sen* has the meaning of "clay"–the very substance from which humankind was said to have been created.

If we accept for a moment that there could be a legitimate relationship between these symbols from the deep storyline of the Dogon and the components of genetic science, then we might be able use that information to identify other mythological symbols from the surface storyline that are less well understood. An example of this is found when we consider the *Anunnaki* or *Anunnaku*, the mysterious ancestral gods of the Sumerians. Robert K. G. Temple says of the *Anunnaki* in his book *The Sirius Mystery*:

> "No certain identification of any important Sumerian god with any one of the Anunnaki exists except peripherally . . . In fact, all Sumerologists have been puzzled by the Anunnaki. They have not been 'identified' and no one knows exactly what is meant by them. They recur often throughout the texts, which makes it all the more annoying that nowhere are they explicitly explained. But their apparent importance to the Sumerians cannot be questioned." (*The Sirius Mystery* p. 85)
>
> "Needless to say, none of these seven Anunnaki is ever identified as an individual god . . . No Sumerologist has satisfactorily explained all this. It is terribly imprecise and confusing–unless one had a structure to supply which fits under the cloth and matches the contours and thereby be accepted as a tentative basis of explanation." (*The Sirius Mystery* p. 94)

Other researchers agree about the lack of definition that surrounds the *Anunnaki*. In their book *Gods, Demons and Symbols of Ancient Mesopotamia*, Jeremy Black and Anthony Green touch briefly on the *Anunakki* and define them– as best as is possible–in the following terms:

> "The Anuna (Anunnakku), which possibly means "princely offspring", is used in the earlier, especially Sumerian, texts as a general word for the gods, in particular the early gods who were born first and were

not differentiated with individual names." (*Gods, Demons and Symbols of Ancient Mesopotamia* p.34)

In the Sumerian culture, the *Anunnaki* hold a place that is parallel to that of the *eight ancestors* of the Dogon, who were the predecessors of the eighty descendants of the eight Dogon families. Ancient and modern sources vary regarding the exact number of *Anunnaki*–for instance, in the *Enuma Elish* they are represented as the seven judges of the underworld while other sources cite their number as fifty. This variance in number from seven to fifty might betray an original underlying story similar to that of the Dogon, where eight original ancestors, one of whom was killed, later begat eighty. Another similarity can be found in the Sumerian term *Anunnaki*, which originally referred to the earliest gods, just as the *eight ancestors* designate the earliest Dogon ancestors. Based on the genetic meanings associated with the deep storyline symbols of the Dogon and the identification of the eight ancestors of the surface storyline with *germ cells*, it seems reasonable to infer that the *Annunaki* are also meant to represent *germ cells*–created during the sexual reproductive process of *meiosis*.

The Dogon symbol of the *eight kikinu*, which are described in terms similar to chromosomes and drawn to look like chromosomes, reinforce this same symbolism relating to *ancestors* and *the number eight*. Even the Sumerian term *Anunnaki*, whose derivation we are told is uncertain, bears a resemblance to the Dogon term *kikinu*. The separation of the *kikinu* into two groupings of four "souls" repeats the pattern of the two groups of four germ cells–in a sense reinforcing the definition of this aspect of sexual reproduction.

Modern science has a clear understanding of how a zygote grows and develops into an embryo and then into a fetus. The sperm fertilizes the egg to create the zygote, which initiates the process of growth. Around the third week of development, the spinal cord and the brain emerge, and a rudimentary heart forms. By the fourth week the embryo begins to develop ears and eyes. By the eighth or ninth week the embryo starts to form appendages. By the twelfth or thirteenth week the embryo–now called a fetus–begins to take on the appearance of a baby, complete with recognizable sex organs. In *The Pale Fox*, Griaule and Dieterlen relate what the Dogon say about this same developmental process, and again seem to express themselves in distinctly scientific terms, even as regards the sequence of the stages in which an embryo develops:

" . . . in the first stage, the word in the *sosogu* was androgynous; it was the "life" of the being, still undifferentiated: it was "vegetative life".

"During the following stage, the "word" will be nourished by food, the essence of which will be passed into the blood. It will differentiate itself (into male or female), will take on its character by passing through the internal organs, beginning with the heart, which connects with the suprabranchial organs, thus associating the being's physiology with its psychology. The eighth articulation of the word will be in the sex, the reproductive organ that will permit the adult to give birth to a new being. (*The Pale Fox* p. 165)"

The final four *yala* of the 66 signs in the spiral of *Amma's egg* are explained by Griaule and Dieterlen from a genetic standpoint using the same concepts previously quoted in our discussion of quantum structure to describe the four varieties of quarks:

"The four final *yala* are assigned to the *sene*, here called "testimony of the former world" . . . and of the first genesis. Their number emphasizes the presence in the new universe of the four elements, pre-

served by Amma with the *sene*, in the following order: water, fire, earth and air, the last being located at
the tip of the spiral." (*The Pale Fox* p.123)

The above symbols, which in the first Dogon storyline
represent the building blocks of matter, are intepreted in the
second storyline as representing the building blocks of DNA.
DNA is constructed from components called *nucleotides*.
Every nucleotide is made up of a *phosphate*, and one of
four possible nitrogen bases called *adenine, cyctosine, gua-
nine and thymine*. We recall from our prior discussions of
the *266 seeds of Amma* that the Dogon subclassify these
signs into groups using two different methods. By one method
of groupings were blocks as 6, then 20, then 4 times 40.
The number of signs in these groupings correspond closely
to key numbers relating to DNA. Rush W. Dozier, Jr writes
in **Codes of Evolution**:

> "The genetic code, as we have seen, shapes all life
> on Earth. It consists of a four-letter alphabet made up
> of four different kinds of nucleotides. These nucle-
> otides are the structural units that make up the DNA
> molecule. The sequence of nucleotides on the DNA
> molecule provides all the information needed to
> make a human being or any other organism. A word
> in this alphabet consists of a sequence of three nucle-
> otides and is called a codon. Each codon-word stands
> for one of twenty different amino acids." (*Codes of
> Evolution* p. 7)

The structure of DNA represents one of the ultimate
spiraling coils of creation. Its structure represents a kind of
coiled coil, that culminates in the shape of a spiraling double-
helix. Griaule and Dieterlen convey the creation of the Dogon
equivalent of the double-helix of DNA in familiar scientific
terms. The references in this case are expressed in relation

to the creation of heavenly bodies, but because of the dual plotlines of the Dogon creation story, in this case one set of symbolism applies to both the creation of the universe and to genetic reproduction:

> " . . . this expresses the duality of "Amma's egg" and of the universe in formation–both are 266–for it is said that, while unfolding themselves, the spinning *yala* became twins. The emergence of the *yala* from the spiral crossing the signs of the collateral directions of space prefigured the future creation of all the heavenly bodies. " (*The Pale Fox* p. 126)

Once again, we can see that when we apply the most obvious of meanings–those consistent with the beliefs of the Dogon themselves–to each of the creation symbols associated with *Amma's egg*, what is revealed is specific and accurate information about the science of *genetics*. The information compares favorably to an encyclopedic article on *genetics*, touching on each of the same subject areas, and even providing us with a similar diagram, so recognizable that it hardly requires interpretation. The discussion of *chromosomes* agrees in many details with what science tells us, and the parallels between the *X and Y chromosomes* and the Dogon numerological symbols are so embarrassingly obvious that we can only wonder that it took us so long to notice them.

The dual symbolism of *Amma's egg*, which associates the primordial *quantum forces* of the Big Bang with the *genetic forces* of sexual reproduction, is based on a fundamental equivalence that has not gone unnoticed by modern science. Rush W. Dozier, Jr. writes in **Codes of Evolution:**

> "The quantum code is the most complex and profound model ever produced by the human mind. Its usefulness is unlimited. By grasping the nature of

> atoms and molecules, physics provided the basic in-
> sight into understanding the genetic and synaptic
> codes. For the genetic code is constructed out of
> special kinds of atoms and molecules in the cell, while
> the synaptic code is formed by atoms and molecules
> in the brain." (*Codes of Evolution* p.36)
>
> "All the particles and forces we see today evolved
> from the big bang . . . most physicists believe that there
> was no distinction between particles and forces at the
> big bang. They all blended together into a unified,
> symmetrical whole." (*Codes of Evolution* p. 29)

In an earlier chapter, we identified *Ptah* (or *Pteh*)–the
Egyptian blacksmith, sculptor, and fashioner of man–as another name for *Khnoum* and a likely counterpart to the Dogon
male Nummo. As the ostensible creator of man, we might
expect *Ptah* to be connected in some significant way to the
Dogon symbolism of *genetics and sexual reproduction*. Once
again, such a connection is found in the hieroglyphic characters that comprise his name:

It takes no imagination at all to see the *double helix of
DNA* as the prominent symbol of his name, suggesting again
an almost *formula-like* relationship between the hieroglyphic
characters of the name and the scientific concept represented by the god. What's more, it seems that the figure of
the knotted rope turns up again and again in words relating
human reproduction, making it–like the *hemisphere* and the
square–another likely determinative of scientific meaning in
the hieroglyphic language. A similar hieroglyphic link, both
to the Dogon religion and to the science of *genetics*, can be

found in the name *Nemmhu*, which we said was a synonym for the Egyptian god *Amen* and a close parallel to the Dogon *Nummo* and the Sumerian *Nammu*:

We can see that the hieroglyphic characters that comprise the name of *Nemmhu* retell the full essence of the Dogon story of the creation of man–two entities emerged from water and created man from clay. Our case for a correspondence between the Dogon and Egyptian religions is only made stronger by the ease with which symbols of Dogon science can be found represented in words and concepts of the Egyptian language. Likewise, these correlations tend to show that the symbols of deep science already identified as existing within the Dogon religion had clear and recognizable counterparts in the Egyptian religion.

Chapter 9: Archeology and Dogon Symbols

What the preceding chapters have shown is a consistent and surprisingly high degree of correlation between mythological symbols of the Dogon and Egyptian religions and concepts of science. But although these proposed relationships may seem compelling, they can hardly be taken as credible fact unless we can show that they are also supported by evidence from the archeological record. What these mythological symbols strongly imply is that the creation stories that have survived from various cultures around the world are, in large part, remnants of a single, carefully composed narrative that was meant to serve both as the foundation for an on-going religious tradition and as the structure for eventual scientific learning.

The place to begin an archeological discussion is with the beliefs of the earliest mythologies themselves. There is little question that the earliest texts and myths of the first civilizations almost uniformly state that the skills of civilization were taught to humanity. Each culture in its own way ascribes the rise of civilization to the teachings of its own indiginous gods. The fantastic nature of their descriptions of intervention by these all-powerful gods make such statements difficult to accept at face value, and so modern science has turned to more complex theories of psychology to explain their near-universal appearance around the globe. But there are alternate yet reasonable ways to approach these same statements which may help us make better sense of the message these myths seem to convey.

When my wife was a little girl–perhaps 4 years old–she and her 6-year old brother were playing outside near their house. They lived near a construction site for a college dormitory, and the two children jumped down into a hole that had been excavated for the foundation of the new build-ing. When it came time to leave, my wife realized that she would have to crawl back up the muddy embankment to get out, and she did not want to get her clean new dress dirty. Her older brother, being larger, was able to climb out, and when he realized her dilemma, he went to get help. But during the brief time that he was gone, two college students happened to pass by the site, saw the little girl stuck down in the hole, and lifted her out onto dry ground. When my wife's brother returned he was naturally curious as to how she had been able to get out. She told him that Superman had flown down and rescued her from the hole.

Any adult who might have listened to the facts of this story as told by a 4-year old would have soon realized that Superman could not have flown down and rescued her from the hole. But they would also have been faced with the undeniable fact that she was out of the hole, safe and sound, still wearing her clean, pristine dress, and that she had made it out in a relatively short amount of time. After a little consideration, the conflicting facts of the mystery would no doubt lead the adult to conclude that someone must have helped her out of the hole.

The rise of the Egyptian civilization presents us with a situation that is parallel to the story of the girl and the hole. Credible researchers such as Nicholas Grimal and Sir Wallis Budge have expressed confusion at the very sudden rise of the Egyptian civilization against an archeological backdrop that provides few precedents to account for its rise and little or no record of how it actually emerged. One commentator remarks that at 3500 BC we find no hint of hieroglyphic writing, yet at 3400 BC we find hieroglyphs in full bloom and in perfect form. A similar situation exists with each of the critical skills known to have existed soon after the emer-gence of the Egyptian civilization–agriculture, art, architecture, astronomy and mathematics, to name a few. At 3500 BC we find a tribal culture of hunters and gatherers with only the barest skills of agriculture, stuck in a kind of pre-civilized excavation hole. At 3400 BC we see them standing proudly on the dry ground of civilization, telling us that Superman rescued them, and showing precious few signs of mud on their dress.

Modern archeologists have offered several competing theories for how this might have occurred. The prevailing school of thought simply postulates that a set of ideal conditions must have existed at that time to allow an unprecedented (and unrepeated) renaissance of growth to occur over a seemingly short span of time. During this period, virtually all of the skills required for civilization were perfected simultaneously, and by some chance the archeological record failed to retain evidence of that growth. A second school of thought suggests that the Egyptian culture must be a remnant of an earlier civilization, as yet undiscovered by modern archeology. A third theory states that a hypothetical third party–perhaps a dynastic race–migrated to the region at about that time and brought with it the rudimentary skills of civilization.

Each of these theories suffers from the same unavoidable flaw–due to the sketchy archeological evidence, none of them is supported by the archeological record. But what has not been carefully considered is the possibility that the very lack of an archeological trail is itself evidence of what may actually have occurred, which is precisely what the mythological record consistently testifies did occur: A group of knowledgable teachers may have come on the scene and deliberately helped to pull pre-civilized humanity out of the hole. If this were the case, then we would expect the archeological record to show precisely what it does show: a dramatic, undocumented improvement in the technological skill level of society.

One key drawback to the theory that the skills of civilization were taught to humankind lies in the present inability to identify a credible group that could have acted as teacher. But the lack of a definitive cause has rarely stood in the way of a theory that is meant to define an observable effect. For example, science has long proposed that the magnetic poles of the earth periodically reverse themselves. This theory is based on the position of iron filings in lava flows, which tend to orient themselves to magnetic north. Global changes in the direction of the orientation of these filings lead to the conclusion that the magnetic pole has shifted, even though at the time the theory was proposed, no credible geological mechanism could be suggested to account for it. The similarities between mythologies of ancient cultures present us with this same kind of global effect, and we see culture after culture pointing to the same explicit cause–an organized and informed teacher.

Pretend for a moment that you live in a basement apartment with no windows to the outside. Imagine that as you leave your apartment in the morning to go out into the world, you pass by several other tenants of the same building–some of them coming into the building and some of them going out. You notice that the ones coming in have red cheeks and one of them says to you, "Can you believe this weather?". The ones preparing to go out are wearing winter hats on their heads and boots on their feet. In this circumstance, you don't need to see a thermometer or hear a weather report to know with some certainty that you are about to go out into the cold, because you have the casual testimony of a random set of people, none of whom has a reason to lie to you about the state of the weather. Ancient myths and texts present us with a comparable situation–none of these early cultures has a reason to lie to us about their origins, and virtually all of them are telling us the same thing–that the skills of civilization were taught to humanity. Again, Occam's razor would direct us to the simplest of explanations–that these societies may in fact be telling us the truth.

Over the past few decades there has been much controversy over apparent Dogon knowledge about the star system of Sirius, sparked by Robert K.G.Temple's book **A Sirius Mystery** and based in large part on Marcel Griaule and Germaine Dieterlen's article **A Sudanese Sirius System**. The Dogon priests profess to know about the dwarf star–which modern science calls *Sirius B*–that orbits the sun-like star *Sirius A*. They seem to know that the dwarf star is very small and exceedingly heavy, and the orbital period of Sirius B around Sirius A–approximately 50 years. Early artifacts from Egyptian culture support the parallel relationship we have suggested between Dogon and Egyptian symbols, and underscore the importance of the stars of Sirius in early Egyptian society. In **A History of Ancient Egypt**, Nicholas Grimal tells about a calendar which implies that the Egyptian agricultural cycle, much like that of the Dogon, was oriented to the stars of Sirius:

> "A single text from Djer's [Egypt's second king of the first dynasty] reign has affected the whole chronology of the First Dynasty by raising the question of the type of calendar being used. This text is an ivory tablet on which there is said to be a representation of the dog-star Sirius in the guise of the goddess Sothis, who was depicted in the form of a seated cow bearing between her horns a young plant symbolizing the year . . . This simple sign would seem to indicate that from the reign of Djer onwards the Egyptians had established a link between the heliacal rising [of Sirius] and the beginning of the year–in other words, they had invented the solar calendar." (*A History of Ancient Egypt* p. 51).

An even earlier artifact than the calendar from Djer's reign is the temple to *Neith* mentioned in a previous chapter. Plutarch refers to this same structure as a temple to *Isis*–another name for *Neith*–which Plutarch describes as an al ternate name for the goddess *Ceres*–a known symbol for *Sirius*. Based on this identification of *Neith* and *Isis* with Sirius, we are now in a position to explore what the Egyptian religion may have known about the star system of Sirius, and whether that knowledge corresponds in any way to the scientific data said to be possessed by the Dogon. In Egyptian mythology, the most obvious characteristic of *Isis* was that she was described as being in the constant company of a twin sister named *Nephthys*–much like the actual stars Sirius A and Sirius B. *Isis* was a goddess of light and birth, while *Nephthys* was thought to symbolize darkness and death. These attributes correlate well with the brightness of the star Sirius A and the relative darkness of Sirius B. *Isis* was said to represent things that are *visible*, while *Nephthys* was the symbol of thing that are *invisible*–again in complete agreement with the actual facts of the Sirius star system. Viewed from Earth, Sirius A shines as the brightest of stars, while Sirius B–in the words of Robert K. G. Temple–remains "totally invisible without the aid of a powerful telescope". The Egyptians considered *Nephthys* to be the opposite of *Isis* in every respect–*Isis* stood for growth and vitality, *Nephthys* for dimunition–an apparent reference to the small size of the dwarf star Sirius B. In the Egyptian language, the word *Nephthys* was also used to describe the extreme limits of the Land of Egypt, much as the orbit of Sirius B delineates the limits of the star system of Sirius. In the Egyptian Book of the Dead, *Nephthys* is quoted as saying, "I go round thee to protect thee . . . my strength shall be near thee forever"–again, references to the orbit and density of Sirius B.

Looking to hieroglyphs, we find that we can easily link

Isis and Nephthys to other Dogon concepts related to the stars of Sirius. The Egyptian word *Tuau* means "star of the morning"–a recognizable reference to Sirius. Furthermore, the Egyptian word *Taiu* represents the number *fifty*–the approximate orbital period of Sirius B around Sirius A. Another alternative name in the Egyptian language for Sirius is *Sbait*. Significantly, *Sbaiu nu mu* means "stars of the waters". In this case, it is interesting to note that the suffix *nu mu* is made to represent *water*, just as the Dogon word *Nummo* means *water*. Continuing through the list of Egyptian names for *Isis and Nephthys* we find the word *Aarti*, defined as the "two uraeus goddesses Isis and Nephthys". This title is a variant on the word *aart*, which refers to a "snake goddess". Thus we learn that the uraeus–the figure of the rearing serpent worn prominently by the Pharoah–is meant to represent the stars of Sirius. This same pair of snake goddesses–again specifically representative of *Isis and Nephthys*–are also referred to by the term *Aknuti*, from the same root as the name of the Pharoah *Akhnaton* and the symbol for life *Ankh*. The word *aakhut* and its many homonyms are defined as "wise instructional folk", "a name for Sothis [Sirius]", the "eye of Ra", and a "ram-headed god". *Akeru* is the name of the "ancestor gods of Ra", and *akhabu* means "grain".

Another early artifact of Egyptian archeology is the pyramid, which we have previously associated with the Dogon granary. The Dogon tell us that the granary was meant to embody each of the basic geometric shapes, like the circle and the square. The Great Pyramid has long been of interest to mathematicians, both because of its shape and because of its dimensions. There have been many scholarly studies made of the mathematics of the proportions of the Great Pyramid. One of these studies was conducted by Joseph B. Gill, who writes about the Great Pyramid in **The Great Pyramid Speaks**:

"The perfect combination of form and function was

intentional. Instead of being just a medium containing a message, a repository of knowledge as would
be a library building, behold a medium integrating
the first phase of its message in its exterior dimensions and geometry.

The language of perfection, universal and unchanging, is simply mathematical relationships. How fascinating to think of such unchanging relationships being used! Even the verbal and written language of
mathematics changes, just as the sounds and writing
of any language change. What this means is one plus
one equals two, no matter how it is written or spoken." (*The Great Pyramid Speaks* p.22)

One common theory of mathematicians, derived from
the proportions of the structure, is that the Great Pyramid
represents the earth. In his book **Secrets of the Great Pyramid**, Peter Tompkins ascribes the discovery of the earth-
related mathematical symbolism of the Great Pyramid in the
mid-1800's to a London mathematician named John Taylor:

"A gifted mathematician and amateur astronomer,
Taylor made models to scale of the Pyramid and began to analyze the results from a mathematician's
point of view . . . [He] discovered that if he divided
the perimiter of the Pyramid by twice its height, it
gave him a quotient of 3.144, remarkably close to
the value of *Pi*, which is computed as 3.14159+. In
other words, the height of the Pyramid appeared to
be in relation to the perimeter of its base as the ra-
dius of a circle is to its circumference. This seemed
to Taylor far too extraordinary to attribute to chance,
and he deduced that the Pyramid might have been
specifically intended by its builders to incorporate
the incommensurable value of *Pi*. If so, this was a
demonstration of the advanced knowledge of the

builders . . . Searching for a reason for such a *Pi* proportion in the Pyramid, Taylor concluded that the perimeter might have been intended to represent the circumference of the earth at the equator while the height represented the distance from the earth's center to the pole." (*Secrets of the Great Pyramid* p. 70-72)

This conclusion is in complete agreement with Dogon symbolism for *the granary*, since the Dogon tell us that the circular base represents the sun and the circle at the center of the square flat top represents the moon. *The granary*, which lies between the "sun" and the "moon" could therefore easily represent the earth. Likewise, when the Dogon tell us that the structure of the walls and ceiling of *the granary* represents a reclining woman, they are restating their own symbolism, previously assigned to the earth. In so doing, they establish in our mind an equivalency between the two symbols.

If we pursue the mathematical symbolism that links *the granary* and *the pyramid*, we quickly come to see that there is an underlying mathematical basis to the Dogon creation story itself. Looked at from the right perspective, the episodes and events that take place in the creation story can be seen as a kind of tutorial on math. Some examples of this are:

- The assignment of numerological values within the myth can be seen as a basic exercise in *counting* from one to ten.
- The number *seven*, which the Dogon call the 'number of the individual' because it includes the number of the male (*three*) and the number of the female (*four*), provides an example of *addition*.
- The story about the *eighth ancestor*, who descends to earth out of sequence and angers the *seventh ancestor*

who is ultimately killed, demonstrates that numbers have a proscribed sequence and provides an example of *subtraction.*

- When the myth tells us that the *eight ancestors* were the first of an extended family of *eighty,* we see an example of *multiplication.* The same example is repeated in another form during the discussion of the symbolism of *the granary,* when we are told that the rise and tread of each of the ten steps of four staircases also total 80. This might represent one of two more complex mathematical formulas:

$$((1+1) * 10 * 4) = 80 \text{ or } (2 * 10 * 4) = 80$$

- As the story continues, we are told about the distribution of the *eight heavenly grains* among the eight chambers of the *granary.* This is a clear example of simple *division.*

- The Dogon tell us that the structure of *the granary* presents the basic geometric shapes, which include a circular base that is 20 cubits in diameter and a square flat top that measures 8 cubits per side. From this information, we can show that the circumference of the circular base, which is 64 if we use a rounded value of 3.2 for *Pi,* equals the area of the flat top, calculated as 8 * 8. In these results, we find:

  > The area of the flat top provides an example of the s*quare of a number.*
  > The matching values of circumference and area illustrate the use of a *simple decimal* and demonstrate a knowledge of the value of *Pi.*

- The key numbers presented by the myths—1, 2, 8 and 10—are the basis for both *binary* and *decimal* mathematics.

These examples appear in the logical sequence one might expect from a simple tutorial on mathematics, and include illustrations–and the creation story teller's apparent knowledge of–all of the usual and expected mathematical functions. The interesting structure of *the granary*, which is basically pyramidal in shape, although round at the bottom and flat at the top, could easily provide numerous other examples of higher mathematical and geometric functions.

There are strong associations between the Egyptian pyramids of Giza and the stars of Orion. We also know based on the calendar from Djer's reign that the Egyptian agricultural calendar was controlled by the rising of the star Sirius. Some researchers suggest that the three large pyramids at Giza are positioned to represent the stars of Orion's belt. For the Dogon, the four stars or star-groups associated with the faces of the *granary* , along with Sirius, were used as markers for various phases of the agricultural season. As these stars appeared on the horizon, or passed the point of zenith in the sky, the Dogon knew to initiate the next agricultural step. Marcel Griaule and Germaine Dieterlen write in **The Pale Fox**:

> "The three stars of Orion's Belt, oriented east-west, respectively represent the *nommo die*, the *tityayne* and the sacrificed Nommo, i.e. the guardians of the spiritual principles of the cereal grains that are entrusted to them between the harvest and the following sowing season. These are the stars that are therefore associated with the safekeeping of the grain seeds." (*The Pale Fox* p. 360)
>
> "Recalling the identity between the child and the seed, the symbolism of the Pleiades is comparable to that of the kidneys; these stars are associated with the sowing and the harvest. The figures representing the Pleiades–which are like a "pile of harvested mil-

let"–have nine dots for the "eight grains and the seed of the calabash in the ninth."

"The grouped stars (Pleiades) in the world are proof of the eight grains of Amma which he will give as food (to man)." For these stars represent the seeds that the Smith will bring from the sky to man for the first sowing. Just before the rainy season, the [Pleiades] are not visible . . . Their rising announces the approaching winter season, and preparations are made for sowing. This is determined by the rising of the [Pleiades] on the horizon; one says . . ."the Pleiades appear right on time." The harvesting takes place when they are at their zenith at sunset." (*The Pale Fox* p. 364-365)

The idea that Egyptian symbols were used to represent mathematical concepts is one that has long been accepted by Egyptologists. An excellent example of this kind of symbolic relationship can be found in the *Eye of Ra* symbol, in which each of the component sections of the *Eye* is known to represent a simple fraction.

The basic way in which the symbolism of the *Eye* works is explained by Christian Jacq in **Fascinating Hieroglyphs**:

> "Each part of the eye is worth a fraction. For example, the eyebrow is worth 1/8, the pupil is worth 1/4, the front of the eye is worth 1/2." (*Fascinating Hieroglyphs* p. 129)

According to R.T. Rundle Clark in **Myth and Symbol in Ancient Egypt**, each one of the 6 component parts of the *Eye*, called *the Wedjat*, represents a fraction. The rear of the eye represents 1/16, the coiling tail 1/3, and the base 1/64. He writes:

> "It will be seen that if each part of the *Wedjat* represents a fraction of the descending geometric series 1/2, 1/4, 1/8, etc., put together, they make 63/64, i.e. they approximate to 1." (*Myth and Symbol in Ancient Egypt* p. 225)

Since we already know that the earliest hieroglyphs appeared in an already-mature form and remained remarkably stable throughout the history of Egyptian culture, and that mathematics was one of the earliest advanced skills to be seen in Egyptian culture, then the most obvious conclusion is that this mathematical symbolism of the *Eye of Ra* was a conceptual part of the original symbol. The presumed purpose of the relationship between the symbol and the mathematical concept was either a mnemonic one to help a student remember fractions, or an instructional one to teach fractions, or both. As we think about the development of Egyptian culture, it is hard to imagine that a new civilization for whom written language was just an emerging concept could have had the awareness, impulse, experience, or sophistication to create an image with this kind of complex symbolism attached. One needs only think of the English language to realize how haphazardly a language grows, left to its own natural evolution. On the other hand, it is quite easy to imagine a knowledgeable teacher deliberately creating a symbol of this kind.

Chapter 10: Judaism and Dogon Symbols

Of all of the modern religions of the world, Judaism is one of the oldest and perhaps the least changed over time. By its own reckoning, Judaism is more than 5600 years old, which means that it dates from about the same time period as the ancient Egyptian religion. So it is not surprising that it also shares common rituals, stories and symbols with the Dogon religion. The very fact of these similarities tends to support an interpretation of the Dogon religion as the modern expression of a very ancient tradition. As examples of the most obvious similarities between the two religions, both wear skull caps (the Hebrew word is *kipah*) and both wear prayer shawls (the word in Hebrew is *tallis*). Both practice circumcision, as did the ancient Egyptians. Both induct their male children into the religion when they reach puberty, and both celebrate a jubilee year, which the Dogon call *sigui*, based on a 50-year cycle of renewal. The Dogon state that their *sigui* is based on a 60 year cycle, but the actual practice is observed every 50 years. This difference between word and action is attributed to deliberate obfuscation on the part of the Dogon priests, as a way of disguising an important calculation of their religion. There are other obvious linguistic similarities which tie Judaism to the Dogon religion. For example, the elder priest of the Dogon religion is known by the title of *Hogan*–this correlates well with a priestly class in Judaism known as the *Cohen*. We have mentioned that the original ancestor of one of the revered Dogon tribal families was *Lebe*, a name which is quite similar to that of an honored tribe of Israel known as *Levi*.

The surface creation story of Judaism is told in the book

of *Genesis*, and if we take a close look at the events of that story as told by the Torah, we see that it embraces creational themes already familiar to us from previous discussion. It begins with a self-created god who evokes a series of paired sets of opposites–*heaven and earth, darkness and light, day and night, water and firmament*. As with the Dogon creation story, we can see within the story of *Genesis* an apparent principle of the pairing of male and female, and strong historical connections to the concept of serpents as the bringers of knowledge. Hyde Clarke, the 19th-century scholar, writes in the introduction to his article **Serpent and Siva Worship and Mythology**:

"Mr. Wake's hypothesis is somewhat more explicit. He is of the opinion that "Serpent-Worship, as a developed religious system, originated in Central Asia, the home of the great Scythic stock, from whom sprang all the civilized races of the historical period. These people are the *Adamites*, and their legendary ancestor was at one time regarded as the Great Serpent–his descendants being in a special sense serpent-worshippers."

But Adam, Mr. Wake suggests in another treatise, was not "the name given at first to this mythical father of the race." He suggests that the term was formed by the combination of the primitive Akkadian words AD, father, and DAM, mother. "It would thus," he remarks, "originally express a dual idea, agreeably to the statement in *Genesis* v. 2, that male and female were called 'Adam' . . . When the dual idea expressed in the name was forgotten, Adam became the Great Father; the Great Mother receiving the name of Eve (Havvah), i.e., living or life"–(in Arabic, a serpent) . . . Mr. Wake gives the word *ak* the sense of "root or stem, lineage;" and so Ak-Ad [from which the name of the Akkadian civilization is derived] would mean the sons of Ad or Adam . . . The Parsees of Hindustan have the legend of the great Ab-Ad, the first ancestor of mankind . . . The Arabs also had their ancestor Ad . . . The Egyptians, likewise, venerated a similar divine being, denominated At-um or At-mu, the Father of mankind . . ." (*Siva and Serpent Worship and Mythology* p. ix-x)

There are also hints within Judaism of two original creative powers, much like the *Nummo pair,* and an original pantheon of ancestor-like entities, similar to the Sumerian *Annunakki,* the Egyptian *Ennead,* and the *Dogon ancestors.* Likely links to the idea of ancestral gods come from frequent references within the Torah itself to *Elohim*–a plural Hebrew word which refers to "gods" rather than a singular "god". George Foot Moore explains more about the concept of the *Elohim* in his book **Judaism in the First Centuries of the Christian Era**:

> "If the leaders of Palestinian Jewry had little fear of actual lapse into polytheism and idolatry, they had a greater concern about a defection from the strict monotheistic principle of a different kind, the currency of the belief that there are 'two authorities' [or 'two powers']. The references to this error do not define it. A theory of 'two authorities' might be entertained by thinkers who held that God is the author of good only, and that for the evil in the world another cause must be assumed; or by such as in their thinking so exalted God above the finite as to find it necessary to interpose between God and the world an inferior intermediate power as demiurge; or–as frequently happened– both these motives might concur. "
>
> "The controversy . . . over the unity of the

godhead . . . lies outside our purpose. It is sufficient
to remark that the arguments employed on both sides
are in large part the same as are found earlier in discussions of the 'two powers' . . . they quote the
texts of the Bible which most strongly affirm the sole-
ness of God; and refute the inferences from the plural *elohim* ('God', not 'gods') . . .
That two powers gave the Law and two powers created the world was argued by some from the *elohim*
in Exod. 20, 1 and Gen. 1, 1, taken as a numerical
plural; to which the answer is given that in both cases
the *verbs* of which *elohim* is the subject are in the
singular number." (*Judaism in the First Centuries of
the Christian Era* p. 364-366)

Hints of an original Judaic pantheon, consisting of a single
god but including two law-giving powers and a group of
ancestor-like beings, corresponds with the Dogon creation
story, which defines one monotheistic god (the one true god
Amma), two intermediate agents of Amma *(the Nummo pair)*—
and *eight Dogon ancestor/instructors*. From this perspective, each of the competing arguments within Judaism could
be seen as true, because based on the Dogon pattern it
would have been quite possible to have two original 'law-
giving powers' and yet only 'one God'. Godfrey Higgins,
another nineteenth century author, addresses the issue of
the multiplicity of names for the self-created god of Judaism
in more detail in his epic work **Anacalypsis**, and explains
how this concept of many godlike entities might later have
been transposed into the view of a single, monotheistic god:

"But before I proceed, I must point out an example
of very blameable disingenuousness in every translation of the Bible which I have seen. In the original,
God is called by a variety of names, often the same
as that which the Heathens gave to their Gods. To

disguise this, the translators have availed themselves of a contrivance adopted by the Jews in rendering the Hebrew into Greek, which is to render the word *Ieue*, and several of the other names by which God is called in the Bible, by the word . . . Lord, which signifies one having authority, the sovereign. In this the Jews were justified by the commandment, which forbids the use of the name *Ieue*." (*Anacalypsis* p. 62)

"Perhaps there is not a word in any language about which more has been written than the word Aleim; or, as modern Jews corruptly call it, Elohim . . . the root of the word Aleim, as a verb, or in its verbal form, means to mediate, to interpose for protection, to preserve; and as a noun, a mediator, an inter-poser . . . The Jews have made out that God is called by upwards of thirty names in the Bible . . . the words *ieue-e- aleim* . . . mean *Ieue the preserver,* or the *self-existent preserver*–the word *Ieue*, as we shall afterward find, meaning self-existent . . . Moses himself uses this word Elohim, with verbs and adjectives in the plural . . .

The 26th verse of the first chapter of Genesis completely establishes the plurality of the word Aleim. *And then said Aleim, we will make man in* OUR *image according to* OUR *likeness . . . .* From these different examples it is evident that the God of the Jews had several names, and that these were often the names of the Heathen Gods also. All this has a strong tendency to shew that the Jewish and Gentile systems were, at the bottom, the same . . . It is a very common practice with the priests not always to translate a word, but sometimes to leave it in the original, and sometimes to translate it as it may suit their purpose . . .

Thus they use the *Messiah* or *Anointed* as they find it

best serves their object." (*Anacalypsis* p. 64-71)

As a name for the self-created god of Judaism, the word *Iueu*, or in Christianity *Yahweh*, comes from an anagram of the Hebrew letters *yud, hay, vav and hay*. We may recall that one of the hallmarks of the most ancient religions is that the letter representing the number 10–in Judaism, the letter *Yud*–is also used as a name for god. The Hebrew letters of this anagram, which is considered an unspoken name of god, are the starting letters of the words of a Hebrew phrase that is loosely translated by the inscription found on the Egyptian temple to *Neith*. In **Anacalypsis**, Godfrey Higgens renders this inscription in the same physical form that it appeared on the wall of the temple:

I *Isis* am all that has

been, that is or shall

be; no mortal Man

hath ever

me un-

vei-

le-

d

In addition to this frequently-quoted inscription, Higgins tells us that a second text appeared on the same temple wall which explicitly establishes a connection between *Neith* and the stars of *Sirius*, and between *Sirius* and the start of the calendar year:

> "On the front of the temple of Isis at Sais was this inscription, below that which I have given above: "The fruit which I have brought forth is the 'sun'. This Isis, Plutarch says, is the chaste Minerva, who, without fearing to lose her title of virgin, says she is the mother of the sun. This is the same virgin of the

constellations whom, Eratosthenes says, the learned
of Alexandria call Ceres or Isis, who opened the year
and presided at the bith of the god Day." (*Anacalypsis*
p. 313)

There are also statements by Herodotus which positively
link the Egyptian god *Isis* to *Neith* and *Ceres*. He write in his
History:

> "The Egyptians do not hold a single solemn assem-
> bly, but several in the course of a year. Of these the
> chief, which is better attended than any other, is held
> at the city of Babastis in honor of Diana. The next in
> importance is that which takes place in Busiris, a city
> situated in the very middle of the Delta; it is in honor
> of Isis, who is called in the Greek tongue Demiter
> (Ceres)."

Later in the same work he writes:

> "According to the Egyptians, Apollo and Diana are
> the children of Bacchus and Isis, while Latona is their
> nurse and their preserver. They call Apollo, in their
> language, Horus; Ceres they call Isis; Diana, Bubastis.
> From this Egyptian tradition, and from no other, it
> must be that Aeschylus, the son of Euphorion, took
> the idea, which is found in none of the earlier poets,
> of making Diana the daughter of Ceres."

The Hebrew anagram *yud, hay, vav and hay* firmly links
the self-created god of Judaism to the Egyptian goddess
Neith. But we know that *Neith* herself has already been
specifically associated with the *quantum thread* of the Dogon.
This implies that the original underlying symbolism of the
self-created god of Judaism might well have been the very
same quantum thread. To support this idea, we would need

to find evidence that at the heart of the Judaic concept of god lies the notion of the quantum string as the source of matter. In **Anacalypsis**, Godfrey Higgins provides us with precisely this evidence:

> "The similarity, or rather coincidence, of the Cabalistic, Alexandrian, and Oriental philosophy, will be sufficiently evinced by briefly stating the common tenets in which these different systems agreed; they are as follow: All things are derived by emanation from one principle: and this principle is God. From him a substantial power immediately proceeds, which is the image of God, and the source of all subsequent emanations . . . Matter is nothing more than the most remote effect of the emanative energy of the Deity. The material world receives its form from the immediate agency of powers far beneath the First Source of being." (*Anacalypsis* p. 72-73)

Likewise, if part of the original symbolism of the god of Judaism was to the *quantum thread*, then we would expect to find some reference to the creation of the four categories of quantum particles *earth, water, fire and wind*. Such references can be found within the story of *Genesis* itself, and in **The Book of Jubilees**, which is a more detailed retelling of the story of *Genesis*.

> "On the first day [God] created the tall heavens and the earth and waters and all the spirits who served him; the angels of the presence, the angels of the sanctification, the angels of the spirit of fire, the angels of the spirit of the winds . . . ." (**The Other Bible** p. 11)

Even more to the point, there is a specific tradition within Judaism that assigns the symbolism of *earth, water, wind and fire* to the letters *yud, hay, vav, and hay* themselves, and more importantly, to the concept of the vibrations of matter. Marc-Alain Ouaknin writes in **Symbols of Judaism**:

> "When words, particularly those conveying the names of God, are inscribed upon physical objects of the world, these words send vibrations out into the physical world itself . . . In Judaism, and in particular for the masters of the *kabbalah*, this life vibration is the name of God or the *Tetragrammaton*–the four Hebrew letters forming the biblical proper name of God, which often is inscribed upon physical matter. "
> (*Symbols of Judaism* p. 14)

So we can see once again that what we find at the very heart of the Jewish tradition is the symbol of the quantum thread, associated with the self-created god, giving rise to the symbols of the four types of quantum particles in their expected symbolic form, and once again the clear link is through the goddess *Neith*. Knowing that the Judaic, Egyptian and Dogon religions can be synchronized in this fundamental way places us on a solid footing for comparing various religious rituals between these cultures. One key ritual of Judaism which bears careful comparison to the Dogon is the practice of *circumcision*. Modern Judaism explains the idea of circumcision as a symbol of the covenant between God and the Jewish people. **The Complete Book of Jewish Observance** provides a typical explanation of this practice:

> "Among people that practiced circumcision, the rite was usually performed at puberty. As some psychologists have pointed out, this may have been done to demonstrate the father's and the tribe's power over the son . . . the son learned . . . that he was forever bound to them by an individual convenant . . . The

Jewish child, by contrast, is circumcised on the eighth
day after birth . . . The Jewish child enters the fold of
Judaism at birth. He enters the convenant on the
eighth day of his life. Through this rite, Abraham became party to the convenant. His son Ishmael was
thirteen years old when the commandment was is-
sued and obeyed. Isaac, born later, was circumcised
on the eighth day." (*The Complete Book of Jewish
Observance* p. 219-220 (C) Behrman House,Inc., reprinted with permission, www. behrmanhouse.com)

Although deeper symbolism may have once existed, most
modern discussions of Jewish circumcision provide little detail
to explain the practice. The Dogon, however, do. They
relate the act of circumcision to the trajectory of the orbit of
the dwarf star *Sirius B*, which the Dogon call *Digitaria*, around
its companion star *Sirius A*. Griaule and Dieterlen provide
an explanation for circumcision as the Dogon know it in
their article **A Sudanese Sirius System**, the full text of which
is included in translation in Robert Temple's **The Sirius
Mystery**:

"A figure made out of millet pulp in the room with
the dais in the house of the Hogon of Arou gives an
idea of this trajectory, which is drawn horizontally;
the oval (lengthwise diameter about 100 cm.=40 in.)
contains to the left a small circle, Sirius (S), above
which another circle (DP) with its centre shows
Digitaria in its closest position. At the other end of
the oval a small cluster of dots (DL) represent the
star when it is farthest from Sirius. When Digitaria is
close to Sirius, the latter becomes brighter; when it is
at its most distant from Sirius, Digitaria gives off a
twinkling effect, suggesting several stars to the observer. "

Orbits of Sirius A and B

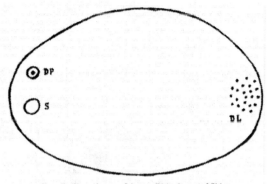

Figure iii. The trajectory of the star Digitaria around Sirius

"This trajectory symbolizes excision and circumcision, an operation which is represented by the closest and furthest passage of Digitaria to Sirius. The left part of the oval is the foreskin (or clitoris), the right part is the knife." (*The Sirius Mystery* p. 40)

We can learn more about the practice and meaning of circumcision by examining the history of its use in Egypt and Africa, since the same ritual appeared in both places. Herodotus, the ancient historian, makes specific reference to the practice of circumcision in his **Histories**:

" . . . the Cholchians, the Egyptians, and the Ethiopians are the only races which from ancient times have practiced circumcision. The Phoenicians and the Syrians of Palestine themselves admit that they adopted the practice from Egypt, and the Syrians who live near the rivers Thermodon and Parthenius learnt it only a short time ago from the Colchians.

No other nations use circumcision, and all these are without doubt following the Egyptian lead. As between the Egyptians and the Ethiopians, I should not like to say which learned from the other, for the custom is evidently a very ancient one; but I have no doubt that all other nations adopted it as a result of their intercourse with Egypt, and in this belief I am strongly supported by the fact that Phoenicians, when they mix in Greek society, drop the Egyptian usage and allow their children to go uncircumcised."

It becomes a simple matter to demonstrate a linguistic link between circumcision as the Egyptians practiced it and the Dogon symbolism which relates it to the stars of *Sirius*. The Egyptian word *Tuau* means "star of the morning"–a reference to bright star of Sirius. *Thaui* was a name for the twin goddesses *Isis and Nephthys–Sirius A and Sirius B*, and *Tua* was the god of circumcision. An alternate name for the Egyptian god of circumcision was *Thesbu*, a word which bears a strong resemblance to *thesmu-tchatcha*, which means "dog-headed" and harkens back once again to Sirius, which was known as the dog-star. Finally, a related Egyptian word *Taiu* represents the number *fifty*, which we recognize as the approximate orbital period of Sirius B around Sirius A.

Another ritual of Judaism, the *jubiliee*, represents a 50-year cycle of renewal and has a great deal in common with the Dogon *sigui*. The **Encyclopedic Dictionary of Judaica** defines *jubilee* as:

"50th year, instituted at close of seven sabbatical cycles. Proclaimed by sounding *shofar* [Ram's horn] on Day of Atonement. Provisions include leaving land fallow, manumission of slaves, remission of debts, and return of all land purchased since previous Jubilee to original owners." (*Encyclopedic Dictionary of Judaica* p.319)

For the Dogon, much of the symbolism of the *sigui* also relates back to the orbits of the binary stars of Sirius. Griaule and Dieterlen tell us that the 50-year cycle of the *sigui* is based on the period of the orbit of Sirius B around Sirius A, which is approximately 50 years. For the Dogon, the complete cycle of this orbit defines a period of renewal, which makes sense if you imagine each of the stars of Sirius returning again to its orbital starting point. Griaule and Dieterlen write in *A Sudanese Sirius System*:

> "Thus the Sirius system is associated with the practices of renovating people, and, consequently . . . with the ceremonies which celebrate the renovation of the world.
>
> The period of the orbit is counted double, that is, one hundred years, because the Siguis are convened in pairs of 'twins', so as to insist on the basic principle of twin-ness. It is for this reason that the trajectory is called *munu*, from the root *monye* 'to reunite', from which the word m*uno* is derived, which is the title given to the dignitary who has celebrated (reunited) the two Siguis."

This apparent connection between the Dogon religion and Judaism based on a common *jubilee* tradition links Judaism back to the Dogon religion a second time by way of the Egyptian religion and our mother goddess *Neith*–the Egyptian counterpart of the *female Nummo*. We may recall that the Egyptian *jubilee* was established by the first king of Egypt, *Aha*, who also founded a temple to *Neith*. Together, these associations establish a firm link between the Dogon *sigui*, and the Egyptian and Jewish *jubilee*s, all apparently stemming from the same original tradition as the Dogon, which was directly linked to the stars of Sirius.

The four Hebrew letters *yud, hay, vav and hay*, act as a kind of bridge for another tradition common to both the Jews and the Dogon–the wearing of prayer shawls. We find a good description of the symbolism of the Jewish *tallis* (some say *tallit*) or prayer shawl in *The Complete Book of Jewish Observance* by Leo Trepp:

"A Tallit may be large or small . . . A Tallit can be of any material, in any color; but it must meet two conditions: it must have four corners, and on each of these corners there must be a symbolic tassel, making four Tzitzit . . . The Tzitzit must be white. They consist of four long strands, looped through a hole in the garment's corner and knotted. In antiquity, by command of Torah, one strand had to be hyacinth-blue. The white stood for purity; the blue for God's heaven . . . Now we take the four strands of the Tzitzit; one of them will be very long, for it will be wrapped about the others. We put the four strands through the hole, seeing to it that, except for the long strand, they extend equally on both sides. Now we have a tassel of eight threads, seven of the same length and a longer one. We make a loop large enough for the corner of the garment to lie flat in it. This is done by a double knot. We now wrap the long strand *seven* times around the others and make a double knot with all of them. We must wrap the long strand *eight* times around the others and again make a double knot with all of them. Next we wrap the long strand *eleven* times around the others and make a double knot with all of them. Finally, we wrap the long strand *thirteen* times around the others and make a double knot with all of them . . . .

Various explanations have been offered for the number of spirals. Adding the first three (7+8+11), we arrive at 26, a numerical value equivalent to the sum of the Hebrew letters in the name of God "YHVH" [*yud hay vav hay*]: 10 + 5 + 5 + 5=26. The Hebrew word *Ehad*–One– has the numerical value of the fourth spiral, 13: 1+ 8 + 4. The sum total of the spirals is, therefore, equivalent to the total in the words: *Adonai Ehad,* God is One . . . The four corners may then call to mind that wherever we may be "in the four corners of the world", our task is clear." (*The Complete Book of Jewish Observance* p. 28-30 (C) Behrman House, Inc., reprinted with permission, www. behrmanhouse.com)

In these descriptions of the symbolism of the *tallis* and the *jubilee* we find many of the key symbols of the Dogon religion. The four corners of the *tallis* repeat the symbolism of the four corners of *Amma's egg*, which represent the cardinal directions of the universe. The wrapping of the *tzitzit* in spirals repeats the Dogon symbol of spiraling coils. The double knot and the eight strands repeat the numbers of the Dogon creation story *two and eight*. The 50-year *jubilee* is observed with the blowing of the *shofar,* which is a *Ram's horn*–again reminiscent of the *Ram* of the Dogon. Moreover, the Hebrew anagram *yud, hay, vav and hay,*– central to the symbolism of both the *tallis* and the *jubilee*– lead directly back to the Egyptian goddess *Neith*–the pivotal link between the Dogon, Egyptian and Jewish religions. Finally, the 50-year *jubilee* cycle in Judaism is the same as the 50-year Dogon *sigui,* which brings us back to the orbital period of Sirius.

Leo Trepp mentions in ***The Complete Book of Jewish Observance*** that the reason for the rules relating to the making and wearing of *tefillin* were unknown to the Rabbis. But if we consider the use of the *tallis* and *tefillin* in Judaism in the context of the symbolic structure we have previously defined for Egyptian science, then ritual practices fall into a neat and understandable package. We can see the *kepah* as the symbol of the hemisphere–a determinative indicating that we are talking about the structure of matter. Likewise, the square boxes tied to the forehead and arm tell us that we are also talking about the structure of space-time. The *tallis* represents the four cardinal points–i.e. the four visible dimensions of space-time. The leather straps used to attach the box to the forehead are tied in a square knot, with the ends of the straps hanging down along either side of the torso. As a whole, these straps form the diagram of the "looped" quantum string intersection. Likewise, the leather arm strap is wound seven times around the arm, once for each of the seven wrapped, unseen dimensions. It is then wrapped around the hand and looped around the fingers to form the Hebrew letter *shin*–meaning *seven*. But in so doing, they have also formed an X–the diagram of the X type of quantum string intersection. The fringes of the *tallis* are tied in loops and knots that repeat the shape of the complex quantum string interaction and hang together to form a kind of membrane. The entire set of rituals appears in the context of a seven-day cycle, calling to mind the seven Cabali-Yau stages of the vibrating quantum string, and are presented in front of and upon an altar called a *bimah*–similar to the Dogon *bummo* and the Egyptian *bu maa*. This altar mimics the shape of the Dogon granary and *Amma's egg*–symbols of the unformed universe–and includes an *ark* to house the *Torah*, which takes the form of a spiraling coil. During the course of the services, the *ark* is opened, the spiraling *Torah* comes out and is unrolled. Taken in this context, the prayer service of Judaism can be seen as a daily re-enactment of the creation of the universe and of the structure of matter–or as the symbolism is expressed by Judaism itself–a re-enactment of *Genesis*.

There is also clear evidence to connect symbols such as the *tefillin* to possible counterparts in the religions of Africa. Marc-Alain Ouaknin writes:

> "The ritual of the *tefillin* carries with it the idea of
> *zikaron*, memory and memorial. The four texts of
> the *tefillin* all express the idea of this "memorial"
> between the eyes. But the second text uses the

mysterious word *Totafot* instead of *zikaron*–mysterious because it is not a Hebrew word. Rashi has ascertained that *Totafot* is a word . . . from Africa! *Tot* means "two" as docs *fot* in an African language.
Why is the word "memory" written in a foreign language, in this case in an African language?" (*Symbols of Judaism* p. 20)

Another obvious similarity between Judaism and the religion of the Dogon is found in the concept of *the Word*. George Foot Moore provides a clear explanation of the Judaic concept of *the Word* in *Judaism*:

"The fiats of God in the first chapter of Genesis are creative forces: 'God said, Let there be light, and light came into being,' and so throughout.
'By the word of the Lord the heavens were made, and by the breath of his mouth all of their host . . .' (Psalm 33, 6, 9). The word of God is sometimes vividly personified . . . but it is an error to see in such personification an approach to personalization. Nowhere either in the Bible or in the extra- canonical literature of the Jews is the word of God a personal agent or on the way to become such . . . the 'word of God' in Hebrew scriptures is the medium or instrumentality of revelation of or communication with men . . ." (*Judaism* p. 415-418)

In Moore's explanation the concept of *the Word* contains many of the familiar elements of the Dogon, including the water-inspired connection between *speech and breath*, and the notion of *the word* as the conveyor of instructional concepts to man. As we have shown before with Dogon symbols linked with the mindset of *bummo, yala, tonu and toy*, the symbol of *the Word* in Judaism is perceived by

Moore as being somehow more than a concept, but less than a fully personified entity.

Once we understand that we can correlate many of the central symbols of Judaism with those of ancient Egypt, then it becomes possible to use those correlations as a basis for understanding other central terms of Judaism, such as the Judaic concept of an *unspoken or unpronouncable name of god*. This name is written with the four familiar Hebrew letters *yud, hay, vav and hay*, which are symbolic of four fundamental building blocks of matter. It is easy to see how the word *YHVH* could come to represent an unspoken name for god because it may never have actually been intended to represent a word in a spoken language. Rather, it seems to have been meant to stand for a conceptual "word" in the woven language of matter from which the universe is formed. Likewise, it is easy to see how the Hebrew word *adonai* could have come to serve as a spoken substitute for *YHVH* because *adonai* means "universe". In a similar fashion, the Judaic concept of a *hidden name of god* might be understood as the counterpart to the name of the Egyptian "hidden god" *Amen*. The twist may have been that it was called the "hidden name of god" because it meant "hidden". Essentially, the name seems to have been "hidden in plain sight", since it appears prominently at the end of every Hebrew prayer.

There are other similarities between Judaism and the Dogon religion relating to the original creation that are worthy of note. Just as the Dogon *egg of Amma* contained the *266 signs or seeds* of creation, there is a belief in Judaism that God's original creation included the *22 letters of the Hebrew alphabet*–a belief which we recall is typical of the earliest religions. We may also recall that in the Dogon tradition there were certain religious concepts relating to the original creation of the *po* of which it was forbidden by certain classes of person to speak. George Foot Moore tells us that a similar prohibition is true of Judaism:

"Besides the public teaching of the school and syna-
gogue, the first chapter of Genesis became the subject, or at least the starting point, of cosmogonic or
cosmological speculations which were carefully
guarded from publicity. The name for this esoteric
doctrine was Ma'aseh Bereshit, 'The Work of Creation', and in the Mishnah it is forbidden to expound
it except privately to a single auditor. The restriction,
which is made on the authority of Deut. 4, 32, does
not apply to the exposition of what took place on
the six days of creation, nor to what is within the
expanse of heaven. But what was before the first
creative day, or what is above, beneath, before, behind, it is forbidden to teach in public . . . Against
such speculations Sirach had given a warning which
is quoted in the Talmud in this connection thus: 'D o
not inquire into what is beyond thine understanding,
and do not investigate what is hidden from thee.
Reflect on things that are permitted to thee; thou
hast nothing to do with the study of mysteries.'"
(*Judaism* p. 383)

Chapter 11: Light

No discussion of the formation of the universe would be complete without consideration of the nature of light and its relationship to time and matter. Science tells us that the unformed universe–like a black hole–was so unimaginably dense that even light itself could not escape its gravitational pull. So we can essentially think of light itself as having been created at the time of the Big Bang. The Dogon creation myths are in agreement with science on this point– they tell us that *Amma's egg* was formed prior to the existence of light, and that it was the "opening of Amma's eyes"–the Dogon equivalent of the Big Bang–which was responsible for the creation of light. Since the concept of light is so intimately connected with the formation of the universe, we would expect to find references within the Dogon creation myths to light and its basic properties. Once again, this is precisely what we find.

Passages which may pertain to light and its properties are found in Chapter 2 of **The Pale Fox**, which is entitled "Ogo". *Ogo* is the name of a mythological Dogon character who imagined himself to be the equal of *Amma* and who aspired to create his own universe. For the purposes of this interpretation, *Ogo* should be considered to be the Dogon symbol for *light*. The word *Ogo* is an appropriate name for the symbolic counterpart of light because of its linguistic similarities to words pertaining to sight, such as the Spanish word for eye–*ojo*–, the German word for eyes–*augen*, and the Egyptian word for light *aakhu*. The importance of the episode of *Ogo* within the Dogon religion is underscored by the appearance of the word *ogo* as the three central letters of the word *Dogon* itself, and as the prefix of the name of Marcel Griaule's instructor priest, *Ogotemmeli.*

As the Dogon describe him, there are many different attributes of *Ogo* which link him to the concept of light. To understand these links, we must first understand something about the nature of light and its properties. The emission of light is closely related to electrons and the way in which they orbit in an atom. Electrons are restricted to specific orbits around a nucleus called *orbitals,* and an electron re- quires a specific amount of energy to remain in any given orbital. Lower orbitals require less energy than higher orbit- als. For an electron to change orbitals, it needs to either acquire or release energy, usually as a result of collisions with other electrons. When an "excited" electron–one with more energy–loses energy and drops to a lower orbital, light can be emitted at a frequency determined by the amount of energy released. Since orbitals require specific amounts of energy, light is emitted in corresponding *quantum* units or packets.

The form of light that we observe most frequently is called *incandescent light,* or light whose energy comes from heat.

Just as the scientific concept of the emission of light is related to the excitement and movement of electrons, the Dogon description also begins by explicity associating *Ogo* with the *sene seed*–the Dogon symbol previously identified with the electron. Likewise for the Dogon, the first signifi- cant attribute of *Ogo* is his excitability and motion.

> "Like his 'twin' brothers, Ogo was attached to his formed placenta as a complete being . . . But he was still alone . . . Ogo demonstrated his anxiety and im- patience. Although Amma wanted to form his female twin and give her to him, as he had done with his twin brothers, Ogo, in his anguish and desire to pos- sess her, believed that she would not be given to

him and he became incessantly restless. Thinking he was to be deprived of her, he 'was irritating' Amma by moving about."

"Now, the lower part of Ogo's placenta was located in the same place where once the *sene* seed had been made. He wanted first of all to gain access to the first thing Amma had created and judged complete enough to entrust it with a creative mission. Ogo "touched" the *sene*, thinking he would find his own female twin in the place where the seed had been produced. But Amma had taken the creative function away from the *sene*; because of its failure it was now nothing more than a "germ".

Nevertheless, Ogo tried to seize it, and he demonstrated his aggressiveness in that he himself did not want to be "touched" by the *sene* seed. They fought, and it is said that during this fight Ogo took away two of the *sene's* elements, water and fire, leaving it only air and earth. " (*The Pale Fox* p. 198-199)

From the viewpoint of science, it is a reduction in the energy level of an electron which causes two effects—a change in the electromagnetically-controlled orbit of the electron and the release of energy in the form of light. Since the emission of light is so closely linked to these two results, we would expect any Dogon discussion of light to address similar effects, and in fact it does. The above Dogon passages are a metaphoric discussion of the collision of electrons within an atom. The consequences of these collisions is that *Ogo* (the symbol for light) takes away from the *sene* (the symbol for an electron) the mythological elements of *water* (the symbol of the electromagnetic force) and *fire* (in this case the symbol for energy).

Our study thus far has led us to believe that the concepts of science which are reflected in Dogon symbols should also be found in the symbols of ancient Egypt. We have already equated the Dogon symbol for the electron–the *sene*– with the Egyptian word *sen*. It would go a long way toward confirming our theory if we were also to find the Egyptian concept of the emission of light linked to this same symbol for the electron. Once again when we look to Wallis Budge's hieroglyphic dictionary, what we find is the word *senk* which means "rays of light". Moreover, the word *senk* is dominated by hieroglyphic symbols which we have already associated with atomic science and electrons. An alternate reading of this word might be "the binding of an electromagnetic orbit releases thee", referring to "rays of light".

After explaining the mechanics of the emission of light, a typical encyclopedia article moves on to a discussion of the measurement of incandescent light. Most explain that incandescent light is measured against a theoretical model called a "black body"–an idealized source of incandescent light whose properties of emission do not depend on the attributes of the material it comes from. Dogon mythology also measures the creation of *Ogo* against a theoretical–in essence, impossible–standard, very much like science's "black body".

> "So, Ogo had travelled around the universe to "see" the bounds of creation. Having completed his journey and finding himself at the center of Amma's womb, he declared that "he knew just as much as Amma" and that he was capable, in his turn, of creat-

ing a world. So he said: "Amma, I have seen the
world that you created." Amma answered him: "As I
have created, create (something yourself) neither in
the sun nor in the shade; you stay there; as for me, I
will come to find (us) together." Amma said this to
confuse him and to ask something of him that was
impossible to accomplish." (*The Pale Fox* p. 201)

Amma's 'impossible place' that is 'neither in the sun
nor in the shade' is the same as science's theoretical *black
body*–a standard by which we are to measure the 'creation' of *Ogo*, or *incandescent light.*

Another key property of light is its ability to be refracted
into a spectrum of different frequencies, which we see as
the colors of the rainbow. Refraction occurs as light passes
through different media. The change in media has an effect
on the frequency of the light, and therefore on the color of
visible light that we see. If light hits the media at an angle,
then several different frequencies of light can be produced,
resulting in what we see as a rainbow. To describe this
same phenomenon of light travelling at an angle and producing a spectrum of color, the Dogon tell about a mythical
journey of *Ogo*:

" . . . Ogo started from the east, traveled towards
the south, then went west and north in the opposite
of Amma who, starting from the east, had begun the
world in the north. Having thus begun his course in
the opposite direction to the one followed by Amma,
Ogo then turned in the same direction as Amma,
thus completing a second path inside the first and
tracing two lozenge contours, one inside the other . . .
These comings and goings "striped" his placenta as
well as Ogo himself, who still bears the lines: three
on the body and four on the face . . . the lines are as
follows:

body lines: red, white, black
face lines: gray, yellow, green, blue
(*The Pale Fox* p. 200-201)

Although there are many different frequencies of radiation in the full electromagnectic spectrum, the human eye is only capable of seeing a portion of that spectrum, which we call *visible light*. In everyday usage, the term *light* refers only to the portion of the spectrum that people are able to perceive. In a similar fashion, Dogon mythology tells us that *Ogo* is meant to represent only the visible spectrum of light.

> " . . . Amma feared that Ogo might be able to make a world just as he himself was making one . . . Irritated by this success, Amma cut off a part of his tongue, or more precisely, "the vein of his tongue". So Ogo was deprived of the full pitch of his voice, thus of the range of sounds he was able to emit."
> (*The Pale Fox* p. 202)

If our identification of *Ogo* as *light* is correct, then it makes sense that in one context his *female twin* must be *time*, because we know about the special and inherent link in quantum science between *light and time*. Stephen Hawking explains this relationship in **A Brief History of Time**:

> "The fundamental postulate of the theory of relativity, as it was called, was that the laws of science should be the same for all freely moving observers, no matter what their speed. This was true for Newton's laws of motion, but now the idea was extended to include . . . the speed of light: all observers should measure the same speed of light, no matter how fast they are moving. This simple idea has some remarkable consequences.

Perhaps the best known are the equivalence of mass and energy, summed up in Einstein's famous equation E=mc2 (where E is energy, m is mass and c is the speed of light), and the law that nothing may travel faster than the speed of light. Because of the equivalence of energy and mass, the energy which an object has due to its motion will add to its mass. In other words, it will make it harder to increase its speed. This effect is only really significant for objects moving at speeds close to the speed of light . . . As an object approaches the speed of light, its mass rises ever more quickly, so it takes more and more energy to speed it up further. It can in fact never reach the speed of light, because by then its mass would have become infinite . . . Only light, or other waves that have no intrinsic mass, can move at the speed of light.

An equally remarkable consequence of relativity is the way it has revolutionized our ideas of space and time. In Newton's theory, if a pulse of light is sent from one place to another, different observers would agree on the time that journey took (since time is absolute), but will not always agree on the distance the light has traveled (since space is not absolute). Since the speed of light is just the distance it has traveled divided by the time it has taken, different observers would measure different speed for the light. In relativity, on the other hand, all observers *must* agree on how fast light travels. They still, however, do not agree on the distance the light has traveled, so they must therefore now also disagree over the time it has taken . . . In other words, the theory of relativity put an end to the idea of absolute time!"
(*A Brief History of Time* p.21)

The consequence of Hawking's statements about the

theory of relativity is that, the faster one goes, the slower time passes. This means that no matter how fast or how long one travels, they can never "catch up" with the speed of light. The Dogon express this very same concept in regard to *Ogo*, whose name in the Dogon language means "quick", and his female twin, *time*:

> "Ogo tore a piece out of the placenta which con-
> tained his female twin in formation . . . He thought
> he would be taking her with him by doing this. Amma,
> however, removing from the placenta the basic spiri-
> tual principle of being in gestation, put it out of his
> reach . . . All Ogo's future attempts will be to look
> for and take back his lost female twin . . . He will
> never find her again." (*The Pale Fox* p. 204)
> "By his act, Ogo was the first to determine a series
> of sequences which prefigure, in their reality, both
> dimension . . . and time . . ." (*The Pale Fox* p. 201)

Once again, we can see that the Dogon symbolism touches on each of the salient scientific attributes of *light*. By following the encyclopedia article, we have been led specifically and directly to the meaning of symbol after symbol relating to *Ogo*.

Chapter 12: Global Signs of the Serpent Religion

Close study of the Dogon religion has given us an understanding of and appreciation for the remarkable organization and design of the Dogon and Egyptian creation traditions. But perhaps equally impressive is the degree to which the details of this design spread to virtually all corners of the ancient world. Recent archeological discoveries now date the earliest appearances of civilized communities in the New World to approximately the same era as Mesopotamia and Egypt, and there is little doubt that organized society first appeared in China at about the same time. This kind of synchronicity in the rise of human civilization from continent to continent lends creedence to the suggestion of a common origin for the earliest mythological religions. Likewise, the existence of common mythological symbols among the earliest of these civilizations strongly supports this same suggestion. If we simply follow the familiar symbols and themes of the Dogon creation story as we know them, we will see that the same myths, icons and idols form the basis of creation traditions from widely divergent regions of the world. Just as the symbol of *Amma's egg* serves as the starting point for each of the themes of the Dogon creation myth, so it also forms the basis of many other mythological traditions starting in India, continuing to Eastern Asia and extending eastward into the Pacific Ocean.

" Brahma, according to the Hindu mythology, was
the creator and director of the universe. He was the

father of gods and humans alike, and in classical Indian thought, he forms a trinity with *VISHNU* and
SHIVA . . . While the god Brahma meditated, he produced all the material elements of the universe and
the concepts that enabled human beings to understand them . . . [One] creation myth describes how,
in the beginning, the universe was shrouded in darkness. Eventually, a seed floating in the cosmic ocean
gave rise to a beautiful, shining egg. According to the
sacred texts known as the *Laws of Manu*,
"In this egg the blessed one remained a whole year,
then of himself, by the effort of his thought only, he
divided the egg in two." From the two halves, he
made heaven, the celestial sphere, and earth, the
material sphere. Between the two halves of the egg
he placed the air, the eight cardinal points and the
eternal abodes of the waters . . . The egg finally revealed Brahma the god, who divided himself into
two people, a male and a female. In due course,
these two beings gave rise to the whole of the rest
of creation." (*The Ultimate Encyclopedia of Mythology* p. 356)

Although specific details of the Hindu creation tradition
vary from the Dogon, the major themes are wholly apparent–an egg emerges from the waters of chaos. The name of
the deity *Manu* is an anagram of the Sumerian *Nammu*, which
is the Dogon *Nummo*. The opening of the egg establishes
the four cardinal points of space and time, and results in the
creation of paired opposite entities. A man and a woman
are created who become the ancestors of humankind. The
elements of this same tradition, in somewhat altered form,
make up the basis of an East Asian creation tradition:

"Myths of the creation of the world begin with emp-
tiness, darkness, a floating, drifting lack of form or a

fathomless expanse of water. Out of this dim swirl comes a more tangible object which holds the promise of both solid land and human life. The egg is a potent symbol of creation, and features in mythologies all over the world, including those of China and Southeast Asia. According to the folklore of the Iban in Borneo, the world began with two spirits floating like birds on the ocean, who created the earth and the sky from two eggs. In Sumatra, a primordial blue chicken, Manuk Manuk, laid three eggs, from which hatched the gods who created the world. A Chinese creation myth, which may have originated in Thailand, begins with the duality governing the universe–yin and yang–struggling within the cosmic egg until it splits, and the deity Pangu emerges." (*The Ultimate Encyclopedia of Mythology* p. 444)

Details of the Dogon creation tradition are pervasively echoed as far east from India as Central and South America. We can see them expressed in various ways even within the Mayan creation story, which like the Dogon, includes three separate creational storylines, places emphasis on the importance of the four cardinal points, observes the principle of paired sets of opposites, and assigns mythic symbolism to the concepts of *earth and sky*:

"The *Popol Vuh* has essentially three parts: first, the creation of the earth and its first inhabitants; second, the story of the Hero Twins and their forebears; and third, the legendary history of the founding of the Quiche dynasties . . . ." (*The Gods and Symbols of Ancient Mexico and the Maya* p. 134)

"A widespread characteristic in ancient Aztec thought is the use of paired terms to refer metaphorically to a single concept. One of the best known examples of this is the Nahuatl term *alt-tlachinolli*. Composed of the terms for water (*atl*) and fire (*tlachinolli*), this phrase refers to war, and the words for fire and water themselves are a pair of battling oppositions. In Aztec writing and art, this phrase is usually rendered as a pair of intertwined bands, one delineating fire, the other water." (*The Gods and Symbols of Ancient Mexico and the Maya* p. 41)

"Ancient Mesoamerican peoples widely believed that the cosmic balance of the world rested on the shoulders of four gods situated at the four quarters. For the ancient Maya, this skybearer was glyphically named as Pauahtun." (*The Gods and Symbols of Ancient Mexico and the Maya* p. 132)

The form and sequence in which the mythological gods of Mesoamerica emerged follows the familiar pattern from the Dogon creation story. In one version, it begins with *Ometeotl*, a bisexual god whose name literally means "two god", and who was said to be the master of the "Place of Duality" in the form of two *Nummo-like* gods *Ometecuhtli and Omecihuatl*. This male/female pair, known in some regions as *Oxomoco and Chipactonal*, became the progenitors of the human race and the first ancestral couple. For the Dogon, the first finished creation to emerge from mythological Big Bang at the opening of *Amma's egg* was the *po*, the symbol for the atom. The word *po* is linguistically similar to the name of the emergent Mayan god *Pauahtun*. Traces of the tradition of the *po* can be found in various early cultures, but none is more strikingly similar to the Dogon than the Maori. In his 1963 book **Alpha: The Myths of Creation** Charles H. Long describes the importance of the word *po*, its meanings and what it symbolized to the Maori, a native tribe of Polynesia:

" . . . the origin of the primordial parents is understood to be the primal chaos in either the form of earth or of a watery chaos. Elsdon Best reports that the Maori have a word, *Po*, which has four interrelated definitions. These definitions are: 1) The period of time prior to the existence of the universe; 2) the period of labor of the earth-mother; 3) the period of time after death; and 4) the spirit world-underworld. This notion of *Po* among the Maori refers to the stuff out of which and the method by which creation comes into being. When the *Po* element is emphasized, the creation is seen as a gradual development from embryonic to mature forms in much the same manner as we saw in the emergence myths. The term *Po* in all of its connotations is a symbol of the earth mother who is before all things, who brings all things into being, nurtures them, and receives them at death . . . One cosmogonic condition or phase resulted in another until they culminated in Earth and Sky, and one of the supernatural offspring of these primal parents became the progenitor of man. Inasmuch as all the foregoing offspring were of the male sex, woman had to be created from the body of Earth Mother ere man could be begotten" (*Alpha: The Myths of Creation* p. 65)

Other aspects of Maori cosmogony are strikingly similar to that of the Dogon. An excellent source of material for comparison to the Dogon is Elsdon Best's **Maori Religion and Mythology**, published in 1924. He writes:

"[The Maori] taught his ideas of cosmogony by means of a singular allegorical myth showing the origin or growth of matter from chaos, or nothingness, and the gradual evolution of light from darkness. The superior version is to the effect that the Supreme Being brought the universe into being . . . Two different aspects of all the superior class of myths were taught.

One of these was . . . never disclosed to the bulk of the people, but retained by the higher grade of . . . experts or priests and by a few others. The other version was that imparted to the people at large, and this, as a rule, was of an inferior nature . . . The former of these versions was that the universe was created by the Supreme Being . . . . A still more popular version, a fireside story, is connected with the origin of land, which . . . is said to have been hauled up by a god or demi-god from the ocean depths . . . The earth and sky appeared from chaos or nothingness–that is, from the condition known to the Maori as the Po, usually rendered by us as "night" or "darkness", but which really implies the unknown. The origin of man is closely connected with cosmogony in Maori myth, for Earth and Sky were the progenitors of the race . . . In any endeavor to obtain information concerning such matters as we are now discussing it is highly important that the inquirer should have access to the learned men of the community, the few who have been carefully trained in the tribal lore. This calls not only for a knowledge of the native tongue, but also for a long residence among them, ere the men of knowledge acquire sufficient confidence in an alien to induce them to impart such knowledge to him. The ordinary folk of any Maori community know but little of these "higher matters . . . One can scarcely peruse any Maori myth or tradition without encountering references to the Po . . . The origin of the primal parents Earth and Sky is often given, as we have noted, in the form of a geneological table of descent from original chaos. As given by different tribes these differ considerably. Many of these lists of names commence with that of Te Kore. This word *kore* in the vernacular speech is a common negative form, the gerundial form *korenga* denoting non-existence. In

Tregear's *Maori Comparative Dictionary* we find: Kore: the primal power of the Cosmos, the void or negation; yet containing the potentiality of all things afterwards to come." These terms, then, the Po and the Kore, are the ones most often met with in descriptions of the conditions that existed prior to the appearance of the Earth mother and the Sky Parent." (*Maori Religion and Mythology* p. 32-34)

Even though the Dogon and Maori tribes are separated by thousands of miles, the concept and context of the *po* is virtually the same in both cultures. The Maori confirm that the *po* represents a primary component of matter, which is the visible expression of the force of a mother goddess who gave birth to earth and sky. Egyptian mythology defines this mother goddess as *Neith*, and we know that *Neith* represents the quantum string. From a linguistic standpoint, the primary meanings of the word *po* in each of these three cultures relate to a component of matter and the beginning of time. This agreement between word, symbol, usage and meaning carries with it important implications. First, it shows that whatever influence communicated it between the Dogon and the Maori was not a casual one, because along with the word and symbol we see an intact transplantation of a complex religious tradition. Furthermore, according to both the Dogon and the Maori, the deep symbolism of the *po* was a *secret tradition*, which means that not just any sailor blown off course could have carried it the thousands of miles of distance—it would have had to have been communicated by someone with a sophisticated knowledge of the religion. The presence of the same tradition in two cultures serves as a kind of cross-check on both, since it verifies that the tradition itself has not changed significantly since the time it was transplanted. It also argues against the theory of implanted knowledge that is sometimes used to explain anomolous Dogon scientific symbols, because it would require us to believe that whoever implanted the information with the Dogon also successfully implanted the same information with the Maori, and then at some point in time prior to 1924.

We know from our discussion of the Dogon and Egyptian religions that the concept of the *po* as the atom evolved out of the concept of the *quantum string*, expressed by the Dogon as a *spider* and by the Egyptians as the mother goddess *Neith*. The likely trail of this same symbolism can be found in the earliest mythologies of Mesoamerica:

> "In ancient Mesoamerica, spiders were commonly identified with female goddesses and the earth. At Teotihuacan, an important goddess . . . appears with spiders. It seems that this entity was considered to be a spider earth goddess, much like Spider Grandmother of the contemporary American Southwest . . . In Classis and Postclassic Maya iconography, the old Pauahtun skybearer can appear wearing a spider's web." (*The Gods and Symbols of Ancient Mexico and the Maya* p.156)
>
> "Although [the] term [Great Goddess] is widely used in recent literature, it probably subsumes a number of distinct goddesses . . . Due to the appearance of spiders with this figure, she has been termed the Teotihuacan Spider Woman . . . The significance of this goddess is still unknown." (*The Gods and Symbols of Ancient Mexico and the Maya* p. 162)

These apparent Mayan references to the *po* and the *quantum thread* are supported by their order of appearance and placement within the Mayan creation story, and by their association with the mythological assignments of the cosmic elements *earth and sky*, which we have already associated with *earth, water, fire and wind*–Dogon symbols for the four quantum forces and particle groupings. They identify the Mayan mythology as a direct relation of Dogon mythology.

One dominant symbol of these ancient religions–the serpent–crosses virtually all known borders and boundaries and serves to tie divergent societies together. Students of ancient religion are no doubt familiar with the many forms that the serpent symbol has taken–from the rearing cobra in Egypt, to the feathered serpent in Central and South America, to the dragon in Eastern Asia, to the rattlesnake in North America. In a treatise by Hyde Clarke, published in New York by J.W. Bouten in 1877, entitled **Serpent and Siva Worship and Mythology in Central America, Africa and Asia**, the author writes:

> "In every known country of the ancient world the serpent formed a prominent object of veneration, and made no inconsiderable figure in legendary and astronomical mythology . . . No nations were so geographically remote, or so religiously discordant, but that one– and only one–superstitious characteristic was common to all; that the most civilized and the most barbarous bowed down with the same devotion to the same engrossing deity; and that this deity either was or was *represented by* the same sacred serpent. Its antiquity must be accredited to a period far antedating all history" (*Serpent and Siva Worship and Mythology in Central America, Africa and Asia* p.vi).

The serpent symbol spread its influence across a very wide span of regions, religions and societies, and was most commonly associated with the acquisition of wisdom. In time it came to be an almost standard symbol of kingship and authority. C. Staniland Wake writes in **The Origins of Serpent Worship**:

> "One of the best-known attributes of the serpent is WISDOM. The Hebrew tradition of the fall speaks of

that animal as the most subtile of the beasts of the field; and the founder of Christianity tells his disciples to be as wise as serpents, though as harmless as doves. Among the ancients the serpent was consulted as an oracle, and Maury points out that it played an important part in the life of several celebrated Greek diviners . . . The serpent was associated with Apollo and Athene, the Grecian deities of wisdom, as well as with the Egyptian Kneph (Warburton supposes that the worship of the One God Kneph was changed into that of the dragon or winged-serpent Knuphis), the ram-headed god from whom the Gnostics are sometimes said to have derived their idea of the *Sophia*. This personification of divine wisdom is undoubtedly represented on Gnostic gems under the form of the serpent. In Hindoo mythology there is the same association between the animal and the idea of wisdom. Siva, as Sambhu, is the patron of the Brahmanic order, and, as shown by his being three-eyed, is essentially a god possessing high intellectual attributes. Vishnu also is a god of wisdom, but of the . . . type which is distinctive of the worshippers of truth under its feminine aspect. The connection between wisdom and the serpent is best seen, however, in the Hindu legends as to the Nagas. Mr. Fergusson remarks that "the Naga appears everywhere in the Vaishnava tradition. There is no more common representation of Vishnu than as reposing on the Sesha, the celestial seven-headed snake, contemplating the creation of the world . . . The *Upanishads* refer to the science of the serpents, by which is meant the wisdom of the mysterious Nagas who, according to Buddhistic legend, reside under Mount Meru, and in the waters of the terrestrial world. One of the sacred books of the Tibetan Buddhists is fabled to have been received from the Nagas, who, says Schlagentweit, are "fabulous creatures of the nature of serpents, who occupy a place among the beings superior to man, and are regarded as protectors of the law of Buddha. To these spiritual beings Sakya-muni is said to have taught a more philosophical religious system than to men, who were not sufficiently advanced to understand it at the time of his appearance (Vishnu is often identified with Kneph). So far as this has any historical basis, it can mean only that Gautama taught his most sacred doctrines to the Nagas, or aboriginal serpent- worshippers . . . It would appear, indeed, that according to a Hindu legend, Gautama himself had a serpent-lineage. (*The Origins of Serpent Worship* p. 39-43)

The "serpent-science" of Hindu legend has a curious parallel in Phoenician mythology. The invention of the Phoenician written character is referred to the god Taaut or Thoth, whose snake-symbol bears his name Tet, and is used to represent the ninth letter of the alphabet *teth*, which in the oldest Phoenician character has the form of the snake curling itself up. Philo thus explains the form of the letter *theta*, and that the god from whom it took its name was designated by the Egyptians as a serpent curled up, with its head turned inwards. Philo adds that the letters of the Phoenician alphabet "are those formed by means of serpents; afterward, when they built temples they assigned them a place in the adytums, instituted various ceremonies and solemnities in honor of them, and adored them as the supreme gods, rulers of the universe." Bunsen thinks the sense of this passage is "that the forms and movements of serpents were employed in the invention of the oldest letters, which represent the gods." . . . According to another tradition, the ancient theology of Egypt was said to have been given by the Agathodaemon, who was the benefactor of all mankind . . . Among various African tribes this animal is viewed with great veneration, under the belief that it is often the reembodiment of a deceased ancestor . . . Mr. Squier remarks that "many of the North American tribes entertain a superstitious regard for serpents . . . Charlevoix states that the Natchez had the figure of a rattlesnake, carved from wood, placed among other objects upon the altar of their temple, to which they paid great honor. Heckwelder relates that the Linni Linape called the rattlesnake 'grandfather' and would on no account allow it to be destroyed . . . Carver also mentions an instance of similar regard on the part of a Menominee Indian, who carried a rattlesnake constantly with him, 'treating it as a deity, and calling it his great father' . . . The most curious notion, however, is that of the Mexicans, who always represented the first woman, whose name was translated by the old Spanish writers "the woman of our flesh", as accompanied by a great male serpent. This serpent is the sun-god *Tonacatl-coatl*, the principal deity of the Mexican pantheon, and his female companion, the goddess mother of mankind, has the title *cihua-cohuatl*, which signifies "woman of the serpent." With the Peruvians, also, the principal deity was the serpent-sun, whose wife, the female serpent, gave birth to a boy and a girl from whom all mankind were said to be descended. It is remarkable that the serpent-origin thus ascribed to the human race is not confined to the aborigines of America. According to Herodotus, the primeval mother of the Scyths was a monster, half woman and half serpent. This reminds us of the serpent- parentage ascribed to various personages of classical antiquity." (*The Origins of Serpent Worship* p. 41)

It is obvious from the above passages that the serpent-symbol alone provides a common and compelling link among many of the oldest religions from many different regions of the world. This link becomes even more obvious if we include among our serpent-symbols the *dragons* of Eastern Asia. We can find many familiar Dogon symbols in the following entry on Chinese Dragons from **The Ultimate Encyclopedia of Mythology**:

> "The Chinese Dragon came first in the mythical hierarchy of 360 scaly creatures, and was one of the four animals who symbolized the cardinal points. Associated with the east, the dragon stood for sunrise, spring and fertility and was opposed by the white tiger of the west, who represented death. Daoist dragons were benevolent spirits associated with happiness and prosperity, and were kind to humans. However, when Buddhism became popular, their character was modified by the Indian concept of the naga, which was a more menacing creature. In folk religion, the Long Wang were dragon kings who had authority over life and death because they were responsible for rain, without which life could not continue, and funerals. They were gods of wisdom, strength and goodness." (*The Ultimate Encyclopedia of Mythology* p. 468)

Likewise, Mayan symbolism of the serpent falls into almost direct accord with familiar Dogon mythology, echoing many of the basic Dogon notions about the serpent symbol and its relationship to water and spiraling coils:

> "In religious terms, serpents may have been the most important fauna of Mesoamerica. No single other type of creature receives such elaborate treatment in Sahagun's Florentine Codex . . . Three fundamental

notions accompany the Mesoamerican serpent: one,
that the serpent is water, the conduit of water, or the
bearer of water; two, that its mouth opens to a cave;
and three, that the serpent is the sky . . .
Mesoamerican people believed in serpent deities
from earliest times." (*The Gods and Symbols of Ancient Mexico and the Maya*" p.148-150)

Why the serpent, of all possible creatures, should so
completely dominate all of these ancient cultures is a mystery that has not been adequately explained by historians of
ancient religion. An intuitive answer is that the serpent originally came to prominence in one culture, then spread with a
migrating populace to the other corners of the world. But
for that to be true, the religion must have somehow evolved
to a fairly advanced state in almost complete isolation from
other cultures, then abruptly spread in virtually all directions
leaving few traces of competing lines of development in
any region. Such a theory would leave us to wonder how
the migrating tradition had managed to overspread the various continents, yet leave the indiginous populations geneti-
cally distinct. There have been many different attempts by
various researchers to establish the religion of one region as
the acknowledged predecessor of all others, but such attempts seem to lead to unsupportable contradictions, and
leave us with no clear line of development that can be
traced from one region to the others.

If the omnipresent serpent symbol is a good indicator of
exactly how far the serpent tradition spread geographically,
then so are many of the names by which various cultures
called their deities. In some cases already cited, the similarities between mythological names seem obvious. But many
times even when the association between words seems less
obvious, the etymologies of the names bring us back to
familar roots from the Dogon and Egyptian creation stories,
like *po, menu, min and Dogon*. This constancy in the form

of names of gods and goddesses only lends further evidence to the idea that a single religious tradition somehow communicated itself across oceans and continents to the farthest reaches of the ancient world, and supports the many other conceptual similarities which are shared by many of the earliest creation stories. Godfrey Higgins writes in *Anacalypsis*:

"Buddha is variously pronounced and expressed *Boudh, Bod, Bot, But, Bad, Budd, Buddou, Boutta, Bota, Budso, Pot, Pout, Poti,* and *Pouti.* The Siamese make the final T or D quiescent, and sound the word *Po*; whence the Chinese still further vary it to Pho or Fo. In the Talmudic dialect the name is prounounced *Poden* or *Pooden* . . . [Another] is *Min-Eswara,* formed by the same title *Min* or *Man* or *Menu* joined to *Eswara* . . . [Another] is *Dagon* or *Dagun,* or *Dak-Po* . . . *Wot* or *Vod* is a mere variation of *Bod*; and *Woden* [Odin] is simply the Talmudic mode of pronouncing Buddha . . . ." (*Anacalypsis* p. 153)

"Amon is the *Om* of India, and *On* or..*an* of the Hebrews . . . The word Am, Om, or Um, occurs in many languages, but has generally a meaning some way connected with the idea of a circle or cycle . . . there is a strong probability that the radical meaning of this word is cycle or circle. The name of the Supreme Being among the Brahmins of India is the first syllable only of this word pronounced AM . . . The ancients had a precious stone called Ombria. It was supposed to have descended from heaven . . . The word ON . . . is written in the Old Testament in two ways, *aun* and *an* . . . This word is supposed to mean the sun . . . but I think it only stood for the sun as emblem of the procreative power of nature . . . The word *am* in the Hebrew not only signifies might, strength, power, firmness, solidity, truth, but it means

also *mother,* as in Genesis ii, 24 . . . If the word *am* [is
taken to] mean mother, then a still more recondite
idea will be implied, viz. the mother generative
power, or the maternal generative power. "
(*Anacalypsis* p. 109-110)

Another prominent feature of the Dogon creation story
that is found in many other ancient cultures is that of the
ancestral gods. Dogon myths tell about eight ancestors, one
of whom was later killed, which left seven surviving ancestors. During their instructional sessions, Ogotemmeli carefully explained to Marcel Griaule that the killing of the Dogon
ancestor was only a parable used to illustrate a point–by our
interpretation, the mathematical concept of *subtraction*–and
that no ancestor was actually killed. But the story serves to
explain why some cultures retain a memory of eight ancestor-like gods while others recall only seven. We have already mentioned the *Anunnaki* of the Sumerians, the Egyptian *Ennead,* and the *Elohim* of Judaism as examples of
these ancestor-gods, but there are others which could also
be included, like the *Seven Sages* of the ancient Chinese
tradition.

Another common feature of ancient religions that crosses
all boundaries and borders is that of the pyramid. The pyramid is so thoroughly universal a structure that it almost goes
unnoticed as a symbol that must have been somehow transmitted from region to region. Pyramids are found in many
different regions of the world, including the famous peaked
pyramids of Giza and the well-known flat-topped pyramids
of Mexico and Central America. Less well known are the
many pyramids found in Eastern Asia and China. Some include among the ranks of pyramidal structures the ancient
mounds of the British Isles and North America. Much of the
Dogon symbolism of the *granary* is reflected in pyramids of
other regions, including the association of its faces with the
star groups of Orion, the Pleiades, and Venus. For the Dogon,

the stars of Orion were the guardians of the grains, and so watched over the harvest. There are several current theories linking the stars of Orion with the Egyptian pyramids at Giza. For the Dogon, the *granary*–like the earth–represents a woman lying on her back with her knees up. Similar symbolic imagery is used in the Mayan religion to describe a pyramid.

As previously noted, the symbolic relationship between the Dogon *granary* and the earth runs parallel to modern mathematical analysis of the Great Pyramid of Egypt. The recognized mathematical proportions of the Great Pyramid support similar Dogon concepts of the geometric symbolism of the *granary*. In fact, a popular theory holds that the Great Pyramid was built to establish and preserve standard units of measure. Many different sets of calculations have been performed to link the Pyramid to classical units of measure, such as the *cubit* and the *stadium*, and to demonstrate that these units of measure are increments of the actual proportions of the earth–the distance around the equator, the distance from the pole to the equator, or a fraction of a degree of longitude or latitude. The issue of ancient units of measure is quite complex, since it is not possible to discuss the *cubit* without first specifying *the cubit of what culture during what time period*, and would require its own book to do it justice. An exhaustive study of many different ancient units of measure is presented by A.E. Berriman in his work **Historical Metrology**. Without doubt, certain ancient units of measure and their related symbolism attained a near-universal status, such as the names of the days of the week and their relationship to gods of mythology, the astrological signs and their relationship to the constellations and calendar months. Many are founded on base-60 mathematics, as is reflected by the 360-degree circle, the 360-day year of the ancients, the 60-minute hour and the 60-second minute. Indications of this system of measurement are found among

Dogon mythology, and among the mythologies of other cultures around the world.

We have previously discussed the Dogon myth of Ogo in terms of its relationship to the concept of *light*. But this same myth also tells us the history of the foundation of the base-60 system of measurement. *Ogo*'s attempts to explore the boundaries of *Amma's* world represent for the Dogon the first source of these measurements.

> "Dissatisfied and breaking all the rules, Ogo began to move about with the intention of getting hold of the secrets of the universe in formation . . . He began by measuring this universe. To do this, one says, he "walked" inside the womb and took 8,000 x 60 "steps" over sixty periods, the "number" of this placenta. The total obtained, 28,800,000 "steps" will make up the distance that will eventually separate the sky from the Earth, as well as the circumference of the terrestrial world to which Ogo was to be confined . . .
>
> . . . the stripes of the placenta are the prefiguration of the morphology of the terrestrial world to which Ogo will be attached: the Earth will be represented by a rectangle divided into sixty parcels.
>
> So, Ogo had travelled around the universe to "see" the bounds of creation. Having completed his journey and finding himself at the center of Amma's womb, he declared that "he knew just as much as Amma" . . . . Leaving the center where he was, and sent back by Amma to the west . . . he wove a utensil in the form of a bonnet . . . Starting at the top and ending at the bottom, he made it so well, in fact, that, once the object was finished, he found himself enclosed inside, just as Amma had enclosed himself in the primordial egg. This object . . . was round and

> egg-shaped in the image of "Amma's sky" . . . . (*The Pale Fox* p. 200-202)

What the travels of *Ogo* have described–the basket formed with 60 steps over 60 periods–is the familiar grid of the lines of longitude and latitude. This "utensil" is a tool, used by *Ogo* to measure the earth. Knowing that *Ogo* may also be a metaphor for *light*, it is a point of particular interest in Dogon mythology that it is *Ogo* who is chosen to measure the earth, since mankind has discovered in this modern age of lasers that the most precise tool for accurate measurement is *light*.

Another near-universal aspect of the earliest religions is a great preoccupation with and knowledge of astronomy. The advanced state of Egyptian, Chinese, and Mayan astronomical knowledge is well-established fact, and has been linked in many ways in each culture to the pyramid. It was the surprisingly advanced nature of apparent Dogon astronomical knowledge that inspired Robert K.G.Temple's book **The Sirius Mystery** and brought the Dogon tribe into the consciousness of the general public. Each culture was concerned with tracking the movements of the planet Venus, timed their agricultural cycles to the movements of stars and constellations such as Sirius, Orion and the Pleaides, and maintained sophisticated calendars founded on principles of astronomy.

In general, we can see each of these important aspects of Dogon mythology and religion mirrored to a greater or lesser extent in culture after culture from widespread regions of the earth. The similiarities express themselves to such a degree that it is hard not to believe that they started out as part of a single tradition. Dogon mythology may just be one more expression of that tradition, but preserved in such a way that it makes a good template against which to examine the others.

Chapter 13: Connections With Greek Mythology

As we become more familiar with the symbols and stories of the Dogon religion, it is hard not to notice similarities between themes and events in Dogon mythology and those of the more familiar myths of the ancient Greeks. Marcel Griaule himself compared the richness of Dogon mythology to that of Hesiod–the early Greek poet/philosopher. This was no doubt because of the many links he saw between the two mythologies. Likewise, there are many references in Greek philosophy to the "knowledge of the ancients" that bring to mind themes and symbols of the Dogon that are closely entwined with those of the ancient Egyptians. The creation story that has survived from Greek mythology follows the same general storyline as that of the Dogon and includes many of the same symbols. But by the time of the Greeks, much of the richness of detail had been lost from the narrative, and other colorful details added.. Still the story–which is drawn from Hesiod and presented by Edith Hamilton in *Mythology*–remains quite recognizable:

> "Long before the gods appeared, in the dim past, uncounted ages ago, there was only the formless confusion of Chaos brooded over by unbroken darkness. At last, but how no one ever tried to explain, two children were born to the shapeless nothingness. Night was the child of Chaos and so was Erebus, which is the unfathomable depth where death dwells. In the whole universe there was nothing else; all was black, empty, silent, endless.

And then a marvel of marvels came to pass. In some mysterious way, from this horror of blank boundless vacancy the best of all things came into being. A great playwright, the comic poet Aristophanes, describes its coming in words often quoted:–

> . . . Black winged Night
> Into the bosom of Erebus dark and deep
> Laid a wind-born egg, and as the seasons rolled
> Forth sprang Love, the longed-for, shining,
> with wings of gold.

From darkness and from death Love was born, and with its birth, order and beauty began to banish blind confusion. Love created Light with its companion, radiant Day.

What took place next was the creation of the earth, but this, too, no one ever tried to explain. It just happened. With the coming of love and light it seemed natural that the earth also should appear . . . . Earth was the solid ground, yet vaguely a personality, too. Heaven was the blue vault on high, but it acted in some ways as a human being would.

To the people who told these stories all the universe was alive with the same kind of life they knew in themselves. They were individual persons, so they personified everything which had the obvious marks of life, everything which moved and changed: earth in winter and summer; the sky with its shifting stars; the restless sea, and so on. It was only a dim personi-fication; something vague and immense which with its motion brought about change and therefore was alive."

(*Mythology* p. 65-68)

Like many other ancient cultures, the society of ancient Greeks preserved a second creation tradition, and like the first tradition it includes details that are similar to those of the Dogon. Thomas Bulfinch includes a summary of this second storyline in his classic work on Greek mythology, *Age of Fable*:

> "There is another cosmogony, or account of the creation, according to which Earth, Erebus, and Love were the first of beings. Love (Eros) issued from the egg of Night, which floated on Chaos. By his arrows and torch he pierced and vivified all things, producing life and joy.
> Saturn and Rhea were not the only Titans. There were others, whose names were Oceanus, Hyperion, Iapetus, and Ophion, males; and Themis, Mnemosyne, Euronome, females. They are spoken of as the elder gods, whose dominion was afterwards transferred to others. Saturn yielded to Jupiter, Oceanus to Neptune, Hyperion to Apollo. Hyperion was the father of the Sun, Moon and Dawn. He is therefore the original sun-god, and is painted with the splendor and beauty which were afterward bestowed on Apollo." (*Age of Fable* p. 3)

On many points, the Greek creation storylines follow the familiar pattern described earlier in this text, echoing details of the Dogon, Egyptian and Sumerian creation traditions. Both storylines start with an egg floating in chaos, opened in the first storyline by a wind, much like the Dogon. We can see in the first version remnants of a plotline in which pairs of godlike entities are created. In the second storyline, three original deities emerge from chaos, followed by a pantheon of eight ancestor gods. Although diluted and distilled, the parallels in structure between the Greek story and those of other cultures are sufficient to allow an interpretation of the Greek Titans as counterparts to the eight *ancestors* of the Dogon, the *Anunnakki* of Sumer, and the *Ennead* of Egypt.

We have already made reference previously to parallels between some of the myths of the Dogon and stories from Greek mythology. The first connection between the story of Cadmus and the dragon's tooth was made by Robert K. G. Temple in his book **The Sirius Mystery** by way of an Egyptian pun on the words *dragon's tooth* and *serpent god*. This connection is supported and affirmed by our identification of the Greek goddess *Athena* with the Egyptian mother goddess *Neith* and the *female Nummo* of the Dogon. The many similarities between symbols and plot lines, along with the involvement of associated deities point to a direct link between these two mythological stories. In discussion of Dogon symbols as they relate to *quantum particles*, we presumed an equivalence between the story of the Dogon ancestor who stole fire from the *Nummo* for the first *smithy*, and the Greek character *Prometheus*, who was said to have stolen the fire of the gods. The story of *Prometheus* from Bulfinch's **Age of Fable** provides us with other recognizable similarities:

> "Prometheus was one of the Titans, a gigantic race, who inhabited the earth before the creation of man. To him and his brother Epimetheus was committed the office of making man, and providing him and all other animals with the faculties necessary for their preservation. Epimetheus undertook to do this, and Prometheus was to overlook his work, when it was done. Epimetheus accordingly proceeded to bestow upon the different animals the various gifts of courage, strength, swiftness, sagacity; wings to one, claws to another, a shelly covering to a third, etc. But when man came to be provided for, who was to be superior to all other animals, Epimetheus had been so prodigal of his resources that he had nothing left to

bestow upon him. In his perplexity he resorted to his brother Prometheus, who, with the aid of Minerva, went up to heaven, and lighted his torch at the chariot of the sun, and brought down fire to man. With this gift man was more than a match for all other animals. It enabled him to make weapons wherewith to subdue them; tools with which to cultivate the earth; to warm his dwelling, so as to be comparatively independent of climate; and finally to introduce the arts and to coin money, the means of trade and commerce." (*Age of Fable* p. 7-8)

This story of the Greeks, which dates from a period almost 3000 years after the emergence of Sumer and Egypt, still retains many references familiar to us from the Dogon myths, but we can see that is has taken on the attributes of folklore and lost much of the clear and careful trail of symbolism that is so evident in the Dogon rendition. During our previous discussion of *quantum particles*, we suggested a relationship between the *four force-carrying particles*, which the Dogon symbolize as *earth, water, fire and wind*, and references in Greek philosophy to these same elements as the actual building blocks of matter. Aristotle writes in his treatise **Heavens**:

"Bodies are either simple or compounded of such; and by simple bodies I mean those which possess a principle of movement in their own nature, such as fire and earth with their kinds, and whatever is akin to them. Necessarily, then, movements also will be either simple or . . . compound . . . Supposing, then that there is such a thing as simple movement, and that circular movement is an instance of it, then there must necessarily be a simple body which revolves naturally . . .

. . . the body moving with this circular motion which

is unnatural to it is something different from the elements . . . But this cannot be. For if the natural motion is upward, it will be fire or air, and if downward, water or earth."

In **Metaphysics**, Aristotle credits "the ancients"–by which he no doubt means the Egyptians and their contemporaries– as the original source of information about elemental particles and their properties. He also acknowledges that the Greek accounts of the gods originated with these same sources.

"Some think that even the ancients who lived long before the present generation, and first framed accounts of the gods, had a similar view of nature; for they made Ocean and Tethys the parents of creation, and described the oath of the gods as being by water, to which they give the name of Styx; for what is oldest is most honourable, and the most honourable thing is that by which one swears. It may perhaps be uncertain whether this opinion about nature is primitive and ancient, but Thales at any rate is said to have declared himself thus . . . Anaximenes and Diogenes make air prior to water, and the most primary of the simple bodies, while Hippasus of Metapontium and Heraclitus of Ephesus say this of fire, and Empedocles says it of the four elements (adding a fourth–earth–to those which have been named); for these, he says, always remain and do not come to be, except that they come to be more or fewer, being aggregated into one and segregated out of one. Anaxagoras of Clazomenae, who, though older than Empedocles, was later in his philosophical activity, says the principles are infinite in number; for he says almost all the things that are made of parts like themselves, in the manner of water or fire, are . . .

not in any other sense generated or destroyed, but remain eternally." (*Heavens* p. 5)

The Greek symbols—earth, water, fire and wind—can best be understood as remnants of an earlier knowledge derived from the Egyptians, but still expressed by the Dogon almost 2000 years after the Greeks in nearly scientific terms as the metaphors for the actual components of matter. Based on the texts which have survived, we can see that the Greek philosophers retained a sense of some deeper importance to these symbols and a reverence for the ancient knowledge they once represented—thought by Aristotle to have been understood in earlier times, but nearly forgotten by the time of classical Greece.

We can find traces of the four-stage Dogon mindset of *bummo, yala, tonu and toy* in another story from Greek mythology that brings to mind a very similar Dogon myth, in this case in the context of a discussion of human anatomy. Dogon mythology presents the fundamental details of anatomy in much the same way that it described the process for constructing a building. Marcel Griaule writes in **Conversations With Ogotemmeli**:

> "The seventh ancestor . . . brought up the *dougue* stones, putting them in the shape of a stretched-out body. It was like a drawing of a man picked out with stones. The outline was also like the outline of a man's soul which the Nummo makes at every birth . . . He placed the stones one by one, beginning with the one for the head, and with the eight principal stones, one for each ancestor, he marked the joints of the pelvis, the shoulders, the knees, and the elbows. The right-hand side came first; the stones of the four male ancestors were placed at the joints of the pelvis and shoulders, that is, where the limbs had been attached, while the stones of the four female ancestors were

> placed at the other four joints. 'The joints,' said
> Ogotemmeli, 'are the most important part of a man.'
> Next came the stones of secondary importance des-
> ignating the long bones, the vertebral column and
> the ribs." (*Conversations With Ogotemmeli* p.50-51)

Ogotemmeli's stones are laid out like the stones of a
building–first to mark the major features of anatomy, then to
define smaller features in more detail. We can see an aspect
of this same approach to anatomy in the Greek myth of
Pyrrha and Deucalion as Edith Hamilton describes it in her
book **Mythology**:

> "[Pyrrha and Deucalion] heard a voice. "Veil your
> heads and cast behind you the bones of your mother. "
> The commands struck them with horror. Pyrrha said,
> " We dare not do such a thing." Deucalion was forced
> to agree that she was right, but he tried to think out
> what might lie behind the words and suddenly he
> saw their meaning. "Earth is the mother of all," he
> told his wife. "Her bones are the stones. These we
> may cast behind us without doing wrong." So they
> did, and as the stones fell they took human shape."
> (*Mythology* p. 77)

In each of these corresponding stories between the Dogon
and the Greeks, the Greek tale retains a less coherent version of the symbols and themes of the Dogon story. This
might lead us to conclude that the stories and relationships
preserved by Dogon oral tradition represent a version of the
original story that is, in fact, more complete than the surviving Greek myth. This same conclusion can be drawn from
many of our comparisons to the ancient religions of
Mesopotamia and Egypt–because in most cases, the sensible self-reinforcing details which give substance and coherence to the Dogon story are, to a greater or lesser extent,

missing in the related stories of the ancient mythologies. What's more, they are often lacking the original symbol, yet retain the supporting symbol that modified or described it. From a modern perspective, the consequence of these missing elements is to make the stories and symbols of the ancient cultures seem obscure and difficult to understand. But when we use Dogon mythology as a template to give form to the myths, suddenly we are able to make sense of what would otherwise be unintelligible stories.

Chapter 14: Fall of the Serpent Religion

If we accept the many global signs of the serpent religion as an indicator of how far the religion spread geographically, then a natural question arises: What became of the serpent religion itself? The answer to this question may lie with another common mythological storyline found in the serpent-symbolism of many different cultures, both modern and ancient, involving a reversal of fortunes during which the image of the serpents was transformed in the minds of some cultures from that of deified ancestors of veneration to vilified fallen gods. This turnabout of events appears as a persistent theme among the oldest religions of the world. For Marcel Griaule's instructor Ogotemmeli, this episode was of the gravest historical importance, and he described it in detail to Marcel Griaule in one of their instructional sessions:

> "Immediately after the smith, the first ancestor, the
> seven other ancestors descended. The ancestor of
> the leather-workers and the ancestor of the minstrels
> followed in order, each with his tools or instruments,
> and the other after them according to their rank. It
> was then that the incident occurred which was to
> determine the course of the reorganization.
> The eighth ancestor, breaking the order of prece-
> dence, came down before the seventh, the master
> of Speech. The latter was so greatly incensed that,
> on reaching the ground, he turned against the others
> and, in the form of a great serpent, made for the
> granary to take the seeds from it.

According to another version, he bit the skin of the
bellows in order to scatter the seeds which had been
put in it. Others say that he came down at the same
time as the smith in the form of the granary itself.
On the ground he assumed the body of a great serpent, and a quarrel broke out between the two Spirits.
Be that as it may, the smith, in order to rid himself of
an adversary and carry out the great purposes of God,
advised men to kill the snake and eat its body and
give him the head.
'According to others,' said Ogotemmeli, who attached the utmost importance to this turning-point
in the history of the world and was concerned to
make the attitude of the Spirits quite clear, 'according to others the smith, on his arrival, found the men
of the eight families, and set up his smithy in their
midst. When he put down the skins of the bellows,
the great serpent suddenly appeared and fell upon
them, scattering the millet all around. The men, seeing this newcomer and taken aback by its action,
killed it." (*Conversations With Ogotemmeli* p. 45-
46)

Versions of this same event, although in various forms,
appear in the mythologies of many ancient societies. For
the Egyptians, the story seems to describe a turning-point at
the end of the Old Kingdom, when widespread religious
and cultural transition occurred. Some authorities suggest
that there was great upheaval in Egypt at this time, perhaps
connected with the massive eruption of the large volcano
on the island of Thera, the effects of which some speculate
may account for the stories of the 10 plagues of Egypt at the
time of the Exodus of the Hebrew slaves. An alternate viewpoint, based on controversial theories put forth by Immanuel
Velikovsky in the 1950's, describe a global upheaval at this

same time, the memory and evidence of which is documented in the books **Worlds In Collision** and **Ages In Chaos**. In one of its aspects, this upheaval took the form of tremendous winds, storms, and tides–Velikovsky asserts that it is at this point in history when the words *typhoon, cyclone and hurricane* enter the languages of the various nations of the world. Whatever the cause may have been, at about this time in history Egypt was driven under great duress to free its slaves and make dramatic revisions in its own religion and society. Some authorities cite **The Prophecy of Neferti** as a description of the terrible destruction at this time. The following translation of this narrative is quoted from the book **Ancient Near Eastern Texts** by James B. Pritchard:

> "Behold, it is before thy face! Mayest thou rise up against what is before thee, for, behold, although great men are concerned with the land, what has been done is as what is not done. *Re must begin the foundation (of the earth over again).* The land is completely perished, (so that) no remainder exists, (so that) not (even) the black nail survives from what was fated.
>
> This land is (so) damaged (that) there is no one who is concerned with it, no one who speaks, no one who weeps. How is this land?
>
> The sun disc is covered over. It will not shine (so that) people may see. No one can live when clouds cover over (the sun). Then everybody is deaf for lack of it.
>
> I shall speak of what is before my face; I cannot foretell what has not (yet) come.
>
> The rivers of Egypt are empty, (so that) the water is crossed on foot.
>
> Men seek for water for the ships to sail on it. Its course is (become) a sandbank. The sandbank *is against* the flood; the place of water is *against* the

flood; (*both*) the place of water *and* the sandbank. The south wind will oppose the north wind; the skies are no (longer) in a single wind. A foreign bird will be born in the marshes of the Northland. It has made a nest beside men, and people have let it approach through want of it. Damaged indeed are those good things, those fish-ponds, (where there were) those who clean fish, overflowing with fish and fowl. Everything good is disappeared, and the land is prostrate because of woes from that *food*. . . .

This land is helter-skelter, and no one knows the result which will come about, which is hidden from speech, sight, or hearing. The face is deaf, for silence *confronts*. I show thee the land topsy-turvy. That which never happened has happened . . . .

Re separates himself (from) mankind. If he shines forth, then the hour exists. No one knows when midday falls, for his shadow cannot be distinguished. There is no one bright of face when seeing [him] . . . ." (*Ancient Near-Eastern Texts* p. 445-446)

In **Myth and Symbol in Ancient Egypt**, R.T. Rundle Clark quotes a similar Egyptian myth which tells about this turnabout of the serpents from worship to vilification, which he ascribes to about this same historical time-period—the approximate boundary between the Old and Middle Kingdoms of Egypt. It was a significant reversal that ultimately resulted in the ascendance of the god *Thoth* as the primary state god of Egypt:

"A myth which probably dates from the early Middle Kingdom, describes how the power of the primeval snakes was curtailed.

This God (i.e. Atum) called to Thoth, saying:

'Summon Geb to me, saying, "Come, hurry!"'

So when Geb had come to him, he said:

'Take care of the serpents which are in you. Behold, they showed respect for me while I was down there.

But now you have learned their [real] nature. Proceed to the place where Father Nun is, tell him to keep guard over the serpents, whether in the earth or in the water.

Also you must write it down that it is your task to go wherever your serpents are and say: "See that you do no damage!" They must know that I am still here (in the world) and that I have put a seal upon them. Now their lot is to be in the world for ever. But beware of the magical spells which their mouths know, for Hike is himself therein. But knowledge is in you. It will not come about that I, in my greatness, will have to keep guard over them as I once did, but I will hand them over to your son Osiris so that he can watch over their children and the hearts of their fathers be made to forget. Thus advantage can come from them, out of what they perform for love of the whole world, through the magical power that is in them." (*Myth and Symbol in Ancient Egypt* p. 243-244)

As a consequence of this major episode in the Egyptian culture, the historical reverence of the Egyptians for the serpent-gods ended and a newfound fear of the serpent emerged. Some researchers assign the Exodus of the Jews from Egypt to this same period of time, and there is a linguistic connection that helps to affirm this. In the Egyptian hieroglyphic language, the word *shamash* means "Sirius"– the star associated with the serpent gods–while the word *shamas* means "Firstborn". In Judaism, the 10th plague of the Exodus was *the slaying of the firstborn*. What this implies is that the 10th plague might well refer to this same event and most grievous of plagues for Egypt–the fall of the serpent religion. Rundle Clarke writes:

> "The serpents are the demonic, chaotic powers who dwell in the lower world. As long as the High God dwelt in the Abyss or on earth they were under control, but after the rebellion of mankind he departed to the sky. The serpents thought that God no longer existed and began to show their true colors He therefore sent Geb down to them with a written message. They were to keep within the earth, where they would live eternally. They have power–Hike–but Geb, with his written instructions, has knowledge. This is the oldest statement of the belief that the forces of nature have to be curbed by 'knowlege' . . . Ultimately, the task of curbing the serpents devolves on Osiris. This is a strange statement, because Osiris is usually passive and his theology cannot be reconciled with the concept of nature found in this myth . . . There is an echo of a similar belief in the 'Great Quarrel' where Osiris has to keep in check the denizens of the Underworld."
> (*Myth and Symbol in Ancient Egypt* p.244)

Linguistic analysis provides us with an interesting explanation for another famous episode from the story of the Exodus in which Moses is presented to the Egyptian Pharoah and is said to turn his staff into a serpent.. An alternate interpretation from the Egyptian perspective is that Moses demonstrated that he knew the secrets of the the serpent. In Egyptian hieroglyphic passages in which the Pharoah speaks to the gods or the gods speak to the Pharoah, it is traditional for the passage to begin with a hieroglyph which consists of a *serpent and a staff.*

The fall of the serpent religion has another possible

implication related to the time of the Exodus. If the Exodus was the event that triggered the overthrow of the serpent gods of Egypt, it is completely understandable that the *first commandment* given by God to Moses would have been, "Thou shalt have no other gods before me", since it would have been a specific injuction against the former serpent-gods. It would also explain why this same God would require as tribute the ritual sacrifice of a *Ram*–the very animal that was the symbol or *avatar* of the former god.

As support for the testimony of myth to the dramatic events of the fall of the serpent religion, Michael Rice tells us in **Egypt's Making** about likely physical evidence in Egypt of this same dramatic fall from favor. He says in the context of a discussion about the kings of the First Dynasty of Egypt:

> "At some time after the end of the dynasty all the tombs in which the Kings and high officials were buried, on the escarpment at Saqqara looking down on Memphis, at Abydos, and at Helwan, were destroyed in immense conflagrations. The fires were intense and the destruction of the houses of these great dead was without doubt deliberate. Their memory seems to have been so abominated that all trace of them had to be obliterated. Somehow the customary explanation, of dynastic upheavals and the vindictiveness of their political opponents, seems inadequate for so violent a manifestation of hate and rejection carried out with such ruthless determination over the whole country." (*Egypt's Making* p. 129)

Based on these texts, it is quite easy to see how the serpent, which was eventually relegated in the Egyptian religion to the realm of the underworld, came to represent the fallen angel of Christianity. The symbols of the *Nummo*, now seen in a new context, are also the symbols of the devil in Christendom–a horned former deity with the tail of a serpent. We can even find within Dogon mythology a link to the Christian name of this fallen god–*Satan*, as well as a possible link in the serpent's earlier godlike incarnation to a name for the god of Judaism. It was mentioned in a previous chapter that the Dogon call their creation myth a "history of the universe"–*aduno so tanie*. From a linguistic standpoint, the word *aduno* is remarkably close to the Hebrew word *adonai*, which is used as a name for god; the phrase *so tanie* is similarly close to the name *Satan*. Direct support for this interpretation can be found in **The Book of the Secrets of Enoch**, an alternate scriptural text included in **The Other Bible**, edited by Willis Barnstone:

> "The Devil is the evil spirit of the lower places, a fugitive. He made Sotana from the heavens, so his name was Satomail. Thus he became different from the angels, but his nature did not change his intelligence in regard to understanding right and wrong. Therefore he nurtured thoughts against Adam. He entered his world and seduced Eva but did not touch Adam. I cursed ignorance. But what I had blessed previously, that I did not curse–not man, nor the earth, nor other creatures, but man's evil fruit and works. I said to him 'You are earth, and into the earth from which I took you, you shall go, and I shall not destroy you but send you away from where I placed you."
> (*The Other Bible* p. 6)

In the Americas, the Aztecs tell similar stories of the fall of the serpent god *Quetzalcoatl*, only in this case–like the Dogon–the serpent continues to play the role of an exiled benefactor, and does not become conceptualized as a villain-god who is cast into the underworld. Neil Baldwin provides a summary of this Aztec tale in **Legends of the Plumed Serpent**:

"Every hero must have his downfall . . . every illuminating state of grace requires a dark and cloudy consequence, every benign force engenders an evil one. In the Plumed Serpent's story, the evil force assumed the shape of his own brother, Tezcatlipoca, "Smoking Mirror". He was the h*echicero*, the "somber sorcerer", the adversary "capable of inconceivable deeds" and possessed of "the secret knowledge of the seer", allowing him to cast a spell on his victims. What more threatening name could there be for this doppelganger, this foe of goodness, than the "evil twin", the demonic alter ego of Plumed Serpent?

Some codices say that the resentful Smoking Mirror defeated the good Quetzalcoatl in a "magical duel". Others say the Plumed Serpent was duped into sleeping with his own sister after drinking *pulque* prepared by Smoking Mirror and his cohorts. After a fierce struggle, the beloved ruler of the spirit realm–man of classic Toltec knowledge– was lured into drunkenness and carnality, brought down by the polluting, corrupt, and worldly wiles of the trickster . . .

Like the planet Venus, the sign of his transfiguration in the cosmic cycle–like the very earth itself, passing in and out of rainy and dry seasons–Plumed serpent was fated to die and be reborn over and over again, through eternity.

For now, however, the only path for the victim of temptation was expulsion and exile. Such a dire fate caused deep anxiety among the people Plumed Serpent had so devotedly taught.

"Why do you leave your capital?"

"I go to *Tlapallan*," replied Quetzalcoatl, "from whence I came."

"For what reason?" persisted the enchanters.

"My partner the sun as called me thence," replied Quetzalcoatl.

"Go then, happily," they said, "but leave us the secret of your art, the secret of founding in silver, of working in precious stones and woods, of painting, and of feather-working, and other matters."

Tlapallan is a variant of *Tlili Tlapali*, Nahua for "land of the red and black," the name given to writing, glyphs, and mural paintings.

Learning through these means at the feet of Quetzalcoatl, who possessed sovereignty over intellectual matters, mankind first gained wisdom." (*Legends of the Plumed Serpent* p. 34-35)

No matter which legend of which ancient culture we choose to believe, the pattern of events is consistent and made plainly clear. A knowledgeable godlike teacher, represented by the symbol of the serpent, taught mankind the rudiments of civilization–agriculture, weaving, language, mathematics, science, and the skills of the arts and crafts. After a period of time living amongst them, and having imparted these civilizing skills, the teacher either left or was driven out–an event which is seen by culture after culture as a turning point in the history of the world.

Chapter 15: Concluding Summary

The information presented in the preceding chapters demonstrates a direct relationship between the symbols and themes of the Dogon creation story and known scientific facts. These symbols and themes bear a striking resemblance to those found in the creation stories of many of the most ancient cultures, sufficient to warrant the conclusion that they could represent separate presentations of a single original creation story. The meanings and interpretations proposed in this study for the Dogon symbols are consistent with their known symbolism in the Dogon religion, and with the accepted meanings of their corresponding symbols in other ancient religions. The deeper scientific implications proposed here for the Dogon symbols produce coherent and believable meanings for their symbolic counterparts in the Egyptian and Sumerian religions. These interpretations are often supported linguistically in both the Egyptian and Sumerian cultures, and by the forms of the hieroglyphic characters that comprise their meanings in the Egyptian language.

Many of the scientific facts reflected by the Dogon creation story are of such an advanced nature that it would be unreasonable to suggest that they originated with the emerging civilizations of Sumer or Egypt. Therefore, they can only be remnants of an advanced science of some earlier culture, or else they represent knowledge that was taught to these cultures by a hypothetical third party. Since the archeological record provides little or no evidence of any prior advanced civilization, the implication is that these facts represent taught knowledge, supplied by an informed third party who came suddenly on to the scene. This conclusion is supported by the organization of the symbols themselves, the encyclopedia-like way in which they are presented, and the mythological statements of culture after culture, which declare again and again that the skills of science and civilization were *taught* to mankind.

The Dogon profess knowledge of a number of scientific facts, some of which were not known, and others of which were not even proposed by modern science at the time they were documented in the 1930's, 40's and 50's by Marcel Griaule and Germaine Dieterlen. Because of this, there is little basis for suggesting that the Dogon knowledge is derived from modern sources. Likewise, if the meanings were modern ones, there is little to explain the close correlations between the Dogon stories and symbols and those known to exist 5000 years earlier in the ancient religions of Mesopotamia and Egypt. This is particularly true, since many of the scientific meanings of the Dogon myths are closely tied to the symbols and the way they relate to each other within the creation story narrative. A more consistent conclusion is that the symbols were deliberately organized and encoded by a knowledgable authority sometime before 3400 BC–especially since, in some cases, there is cause to believe that the encoded knowledge may go *beyond* our current level of understanding. There is no question that it did so at the time it was revealed by the Dogon priests to Marcel Griaule.

The symbols as we have explained them represent a complex and well-organized lesson plan, including *dead-on accurate* information about the most salient topics relating to the creation of the universe and matter, the creation of life, and the creation of civilization. The mere choice of a single, managable set of symbols to represent these three complex themes demonstrates the very advanced capabilities of the authority who organized it. These abilities are even more clearly demonstrated by the way in which the symbols support three or more separate storylines, which are them-selves intricately woven into a single narrative—one deliber-ately and carefully designed to serve multiple themes. It is safe to say that these organizational requirements of the Dogon creation story would challenge the skills of even the most capable modern teachers.

Even today, we can see the clear remnants of these symbols and stories in the mythologies of widespread cul-tures from virtually every corner of the world. What this implies is either that the original creation story evolved in one region and then migrated with the populace to the other parts of the world, or else it was deliberately pre-sented in a consistent form in many different areas of the world. Either possibility could be true, and we have little basis for preferring one over the other. However, some of the regionally-specific differences in symbols—such as the selection of the cobra as the serpent-symbol in Egypt as opposed to the rattlesnake in the native religions of the Americas, the use of the Pleiades as a signal for *planting* in one region and for *harvesting* in another—along with wide differences in the names given by various cultures to the "teacher gods", suggest that regionally-specific stories were presented by separate but related groups of teachers. Oth-erwise, the same cultures which so carefully preserved the details of their religion must have all misremembered the name of their teacher, and each sub-culture must have had the same impulse to reassign these symbols to similar plants and animals from their own local environments or alter the timing of their astronomical symbols as the populace moved from locale to locale. Obviously, any author with the knowl-edge and motive to teach these concepts could easily have had the ability to teach them in more than one region of the globe.

Of the countless *apparent* correlations possible in the world, many are rightly and properly assigned by modern science to the realm of coincidence. For instance, two occurrences of a rare disease in a ten-block area of the same city are in all likelihood coincidental. If over a short period of time a third occurrence appears of the same rare disease, it might still be dismissed as a coincidence. But at some point before the tenth instance of the same rare disease, the assumption of coincidence will give way to the suspicion of a pattern, and as a matter of course, science will investigate. The many scientific meanings proposed in this study to explain the symbols of the Dogon creation story began as a series of perceived coincidences, but grew over time into more than a hundred pages of cross-confirming, inter-related symbols and concepts, and as such, present the strongest suggestion of a pattern—one which is quite deserving of investigation.

What is presented here is not merely a large number of correlations. Each correlation relates to the theme of one of three or more stories, and each story runs parallel to each of the other stories. The symbols that define the first story are the same symbols that define each of the other stories. The logic behind the way the symbols are assigned is unimpeachable—each symbol is an appropriate *if not brilliant* choice to represent the set of concepts assigned to it. Prominent real-life examples of each mythological symbol can be found in the environments of the related cultures. Each repetition of a given symbol reinforces prior meanings of the same symbol. The chosen symbols are acutely focused on the themes of their related storylines, so that what emerges, rather than a haphazard assemblage of random meanings, is a coherent set of analogies working toward an organized goal.

When we look at the meanings of symbols that relate to a single scientific topic, there are consistent parallels between the information provided by the creation story and the typical modern encyclopedia article on the same topic that often extend even to the sequence of the subject matter presented. Many times, the information as presented in the creation story could be substituted for the related information in an encyclopedia article without significant effect on the meaning of the article. At times, we have reproduced Dogon drawings to support this information that correspond closely to diagrams from the related encyclopedia article. In all cases, the information presented by the creation story is organized, succinct and correct.

The Dogon symbols relating to atomic structure so thoroughly mimic their scientific counterparts that, if our purpose was to refute their basis in science, we would first need to explain in some believable way the extraordinary coincidence of:

> The *po*, which is defined in terms similar to the *atom*, comprised of the s*ene*, which are described in a form similar to *protons, neutrons, and electrons* and whose "nesting" is recognizable as an *electron orbit*; the *germination of the sene*, which are a match for the four types of *quantum spin particles*; the *spider of the sene* whose threads weave the *266 seeds of Amma* much as the *string theory* tells us all matter is woven from *strings*, and the basic creative impulse from which all of these particles emerged, stated in terms that run parallel to the *four basic quantum forces*.

In each instance where the assigned Dogon symbolism has been tested against related symbols of the Egyptian and Sumerian religions, it provides a clear and coherent insight into the related symbol, even for some symbols with no firmly established modern archeological meaning. When possible, the meanings have been supported by linguistic and hieroglyphic data–again, often providing an understanding of the forms of the hieroglyphs that may not have been previously obvious. Often times, when an Egyptian symbol has an established identity with a later Greek or Roman symbol, attributes of the later symbols support the meanings suggested for the Dogon symbol. The cumulative effect of each of these individual correlations is to provide a cross-confirming lattice of supporting references that clearly validate the proposed meanings for the Dogon symbols.

In example after example, this study has demonstrated a consistent relationship between Dogon symbols and knowledge, correct science, and corresponding symbols and concepts of the ancient Egyptian religion. These examples show that, among other things, the Dogon clearly know:

- The correct attributes of the unformed universe.
- That all matter was created by the opening of the universe.
- That spiraling galaxies of stars were formed when the universe opened.
- That this same event was responsible for the creation of light and time.
- The complex relationship between light and time.
- That matter can behave like a particle or as a wave.
- That sound travels in waves.
- That matter is composed of fundamental components.
- Correct counts of the elements within each component category.
- That the most basic component of matter is a thread.
- That this fundamental thread vibrates.
- That under some conditions threads can form membranes.
- That threads give rise to the four fundamental quantum forces.
- The correct attributes of these four quantum forces.
- The correct attributes of the four types of quantum spin particles.
- The concept of the uncertainty principle.
- That atoms are formed from smaller particles.

- That electrons surround atoms.
- That other component particles make up the nucleus of an atom.
- The correct shape of an electron orbit.
- That electrons can be "stolen" by other atoms to form molecular bond.
- That light is emitted by changes in the energy level of an electron.
- The correct electron structure of water and of copper.
- That hydrogen atoms form pairs.
- That sunlight is the result of the fusion of hydrogen atoms.
- That water goes through phase transitions.
- That the formation of matter is related to phase transitions.
- The correct steps in the natural water cycle.
- That the first single cell emerged spontaneously from water.
- That cells reproduce by mitosis to form two twin cells.
- The correct event sequence during sexual reproduction & embryo growth.
- That female & male contributions are required for sexual reproduction.
- That children inherit genetic characteristics from each parent.
- That there are 22 chromosome pairs.
- That sex is determined by the X and Y chromosomes.
- That chromosomes move apart and spindles form during mitosis.
- The correct shapes and attributes of chromosomes and spindles.
- That sexual reproduction starts with the formation of germ cells.

- That germ cells reproduce by a process unique to themselves.
- That eggs live longer than other cells.
- The correct configuration and attributes of DNA.

The clear implication of these symbols and their meanings as we understand them is that at some point prior to 3400 BC, mankind was the beneficiary of a major "boost up" from the level of an agrarian lifestyle to a more advanced and civilized condition. Although it would obviously be absurd to suggest that the people of 3400 BC were learning advanced theories of genetics and quantum physics at a time when they had hardly mastered the skills of stone masonry, what is believable is that the structures of civilizing knowledge were presented to mankind in a form that would orient us toward a larger understanding of the sciences, and incorporate within its framework generous "hints" about the origins of the universe, the composition of matter, and the reproductive processes of life. These hints were couched in terms that we would be likely to recognize as our knowledge and abilities improved.

Due to the complicated nature of the correlations described in the preceding pages, the compelling parallels between the Dogon structure of matter and those of science and ancient Egypt may not be at first obvious. So I have included the following table of symbols and meanings as a way of summarizing their organization:

Summary Comparison: Structure of Matter

SCIENCE	DOGON MYTHOLOGY	EGYPTIAN MYTHOLOGY
Unformed Universe	**Amma's Egg**	**Benben Stone**
Λ	Λ	Λ
Initiated creation.	Initiated creation.	Initial creation/cosmic egg.
Shaped like a black hole.	Shaped like a black hole.	Shaped like a black hole.
Opens to form universe.	Opens to form universe.	
Creates galaxies/stars.	Creates galaxies/stars.	
Forms bubbles during phase transition.	Forms bubbles during phase transition.	Emergent gods represent phase transitions of water.
Atom	**Po**	**Pau/Pau-t**
Like-elements combine to form matter.	Like-elements combine to form matter.	Egyptian word means "matter/substance".
Proton/Neutron	**Sene Seed**	**Sen**
Combine in nucleus of atom	Comingle at center of po.	Glyphs binding 3 elements
From binding of three quarks.		⊸Ο‖‖
Electron/Orbit	**Sene Seed/"Nest"**	**Aunnu/"Nest"**
Surround the atom.	Surround the po.	
Cross in all directions.	Cross in all directions.	
Diagrammed like four petals of a flower. ✤	Drawn like four petals of a flower. ✤	Glyph drawn like four petals of a flower. ✤
Orbit caused by electro-magnetic force.		Glyph for electro-magnetic force. 〰
Four Spin Categories	**Earth/Water/Wind/Fire**	**Earth/Water/Wind/Fire**
Describe particles w/specific rotational properties.	Drawing of four figures with specific rotational properties.	
Components of matter.	Components of matter.	Components of matter.

Summary Comparison: Structure of Matter

SCIENCE	DOGON MYTHOLOGY	EGYPTIAN MYTHOLOGY
Four Quantum Forces	Bummo/Yala/Tonu/Toy(mu)	Bu Maa/Ahau/Teni/Temau
Gravitational force.	"Draw together"	Orbital glyph ☉
Very hard to detect.	Conceptual stage of creation.	To perceive or examine.
Electromagnetic force.	"Bumpy"	Water glyph . ∿
Orbit defines limit of atom.	Demarcation stones.	Delimitation posts.
atom.		
Weak nuclear force.	"Bows its head".	Clay pot glyph ○
Approximation of particle.	"Approximation"	"Estimate"
Strong nuclear force.	"Stocky".	
Binds atom together.	"Draws" atom.	Drawing board glyph ⌐⌐⌐
Foundation of matter.	Foundation metaphor.	"Laying a foundation in heart".
Quantum String	Thread/"To weave"	"Thread/To Weave/Neith"
Weaves matter. ð✕⌐	Weaves matter.	Weaves matter. ð✕⌐
Forms membranes.	Forms membranes.	
Creates four forces.	Creates four seeds.	Creates four gods/goddesses.
"Mother" of all matter.	Dada means "mother".	Mother goddess.
More Than 200 Particles	266 Fundamental Seeds	
Vibrations form matter.	Vibrations form matter.	"Thread/tremble"
Vibrational diagram.	Vibrational field drawing.	
7D Calabi-Yau Space	7 Vibrations Of Po	
Tears curved space to form	"Breaks through" shell	"To tear/spacious."
new 7D space.	to create new entity.	
Horseshoe diagram of space	Horseshoe glyph.	

The reaction of many mainstream scientists to Robert K.G. Temple's book *The Sirius Mystery* was simply to dismiss his thesis. To these scientists, the most plausible argument was that for a tribal culture like the Dogon with no apparent history of technology, any unexpectedly advanced knowledge must have originated with and been transmitted by some contemporaneous source. This solution to the problem of the Dogon's anomolous astronomical knowledge was considered a viable one, even though no specific person or group could be identified as the source of that knowledge. So when we apply this same reasoning to the infant Egyptian civilization, which emerged abruptly from a tribal culture with no apparent history of technology, it is significant that we have drawn *precisely the same conclusion*–that the knowledge was most likely transmitted by a contemporaneous source. Following that same argument, this conclusion must still be considered a viable one, even though we cannot yet identify a specific source for that knowledge.

As unlikely as the conclusions of this study might seem, they appear more credible than the next most viable theory, which would necessarily assume that the Dogon—within the astoundingly coincidental context of a story of creation—somehow managed to evolve a system of mythological symbols, stories, and drawings which, by pure chance alone, accurately mimic the true underlying scientific structure of both genetic reproduction and of matter.

One of the most reassuring aspects of this study is that its conclusions support both religion and science. These mythologies of the most ancient cultures emerged at a time in history when no discernable schism yet existed between religion and science. The symbols presented here, which I call *mythic science*, constitute the point of origin at which both religion and science began. Based on the nature and meanings of the symbols discussed here, many of the presumptions and beliefs of both religion and science are validated. Also, because the Dogon symbols seem to be the near-universal precursors of many different religions from many different regions, these conclusions cannot be said to favor any single religion over any other. Since the Dogon religion as it is explained by Griaule and Dieterlen is distinctly monotheistic, and given the many intimate links between these early mythologies and later modern religions, we can begin to see that some of the historical charges of paganism made against these earliest religions may well be unfounded.

No doubt this study has not exhausted the limits of knowledge to be gained from the Dogon creation story. Unquestionably, there is more information waiting to be found by some persistent student of multiple disciplines, dedicated enough to invest time and effort to find it, and willing to suspend disbelief long enough to recognize it. The task of uncovering this information may not be an easy one, particularly since there are signs that some of it could go beyond the leading edge of our current knowledge. We can hope that the ample hints incorporated into the story will, as was clearly intended, lead us to the next level of understanding. But as this study shows and the Dogon priests made plainly clear to Marcel Griaule, knowledge waits. It is the job of the student to ask the next question.

Chapter 16: How This Book Came To Be

The unusual subject matter of this book may lead some to wonder how I came to write it. This is especially true, since I am not an anthropologist, I never pursued a serious study of archeology or astrophysics, I have never visited Africa or Egypt, and I am not well versed in ancient languages. By profession I am a software consultant who specializes in writing custom computer programs for businesses. What this means in terms of my daily job is that I am paid to interpret, understand, and maintain old computer programs, and to design and write new programs for a wide variety of companies. The professional skillset which I have acquired while performing my job may seem distantly removed from the study of ancient religious symbols, since my job is sometimes a highly technical one and ancient religions would appear by definition to be inherently primitive. In fact, if you believe that the stories and symbols of the most ancient religions evolved without intentional design over many hundreds or thousands of years, then it is debatable whether my professional skills would have any bearing at all on the subject. On the other hand, if you imagine for moment that any given religious symbol–like a character that forms a hieroglyphic word–was *specifically chosen* to represent its meaning, then my software design skills start to come into play, since one of the most common tasks while writing a computer program involves the deliberate selection of symbols to represent concepts.

In order for one programmer to successfully maintain the work of another, they must first learn to identify the intended meanings of the other programmer's symbols. A good software designer also learns over time to incorporate clues to the meaning of a symbol into the form of the symbol itself. For instance, if a variable in a program is meant to represent an invoice number, the symbol will be easier for another programmer to understand if it is called "INVNO" than if it is calledt "XYZ123". When interpreting a program, if your starting point is merely an abstract symbol–like the letters "STXPCT"–then there could be endless possibilities for what the symbol actually represents. But if you can eventually place the symbol into a context–for instance, if you realize that the field name "STXPCT" is meant to represent the words "state tax percent", then the challenge of interpreting the program becomes much, much easier.

Computer programs are often modified and therefore are subject to change over time. Sometimes a programmer encounters several different copies of what started out to be the same program, and must try to make sense of the different versions. Years ago I developed a programming tool to help me identify and resolve these differences. It prints a side-by-side listing of two programs, comparing each line in one program to its counterpart in the other. Lines which have no exact counterpart are printed in bold face. The finished printout provides me with a conceptual template for comparing the versions–any line printed in regular typeface was most likely a part of the original program. Those printed in boldface were most likely added to one program or removed from the other sometime after the fact. Sometimes a programmer's comment in one version provides information that explains some obscure aspect of another version. Ancient creation stories present us with essentially this same situation–they seem to represent alternate versions of what may have once been a single story. My initial approach to this study was to use what is essentially a programming technique to provide a conceptual framework for understanding the stories by grouping the similarities and highlighting the differences between versions.

When I began my research for this book in 1993, I thought I was simply reading for pleasure. I had purchased a book called **Unexplained** by Jerome Clark, a well-known investigator of anomolous claims, which includes chapters on a variety of intriguing unsolved mysteries. One of these chapters is devoted to a summary of Robert K.G. Temple's work **The Sirius Mystery**, and it piqued my interest so much that I ordered Temple's book. Temple's discussion of the Dogon tribe and their roots as he perceived them in ancient Egypt fit nicely with other recreational reading I had done relating to the Pyramids and the Sphinx. I was also interested in the parallels between Dogon ritual and modern day Judaism, since the Dogon religion includes enticing explanations for the practice of circumcision and the celebration of the jubilee year. I began to let my new reading be guided by sources referenced in Temple's book.

Like many students of ancient religions, my research led me in a variety of directions. I read many books on subjects that were directly related to my topic, such as the emergence of the Egyptian and Sumerian civilizations and the mythologies of Mesopotamia. But questions arose as a consequence of those readings which led me to subjects that were of less obvious value to my main interests. I found myself studying the history of calendars, the origins of the alphabet, and the evolution of numbers. I felt that I needed to know more about basic astronomy and the astronomy of the ancients. It seemed helpful to acquaint myself with the creation stories of various modern religions and the symbols and gods which they celebrate. During this same period I also continued to pursue what I thought was purely recreational reading–for instance, I read **A Brief History of Time** by Stephen Hawking and Immanuel Velikovsky's **Worlds in Collision** and **Ages in Chaos**.

Later I happened across a separate reference to Marcel Griaule's book **Conversations With Ogotemmeli** and ordered it through a book store. Although it is a short book, it provided me with a first-hand account of the Dogon religion and an introduction into the Dogon mindset. After reading it I began to see many parallels between Dogon mythology, Egyptian mythology and Judaism. For instance, I could see that the granary resembled the pyramid, and that the Ram symbol of the Dogon might be related to the Ram's horn of Judaism which is sounded at Rosh Hashana. I had learned that the pyramid of Egypt represented a star, that the Dogon religion centered around the two stars of Sirius, and that the Star of David of Judaism consisted of two interlocked pyramids—or in Egyptian terms, stars.

Many of my sources provided fragmentary references to ancient tablets from Egypt and Sumer, and in some cases I wished that I could read translations of the full text. One book relating to Old Testament documents which I was actively seeking but was unable to find (this was prior to online searches for out-of-print books) was Pritchard's **Ancient Near Eastern Texts**. I had just exhausted all of the possible local sources for the book when a box appeared at my back door. One of my wife's cousins had coincidentally decided to clean house and, knowing of our love of books, unsolicitedly packed up a box of them to send to us. Although he had no knowledge of my interest in ancient religions, he included among them Pritchard's **Ancient Near Eastern Texts**.

One lesson I only learned over time was to question the consensus wisdom of mainstream reference sources. When I expanded my search for parallels of Dogon mythology to the Sumerian religion, I read and believed any number of mythological dictionaries all of which agreed that the earliest gods of the Sumerian creation tradition were *An, Enlil, and Enki*. I had hoped to find a match for the *Nummo* of Dogon tradition, but was forced to concede that I would not find it—until I read Annie Caubet and Patrick Pouyssegur's book *The Ancient Near East*, which explained about an earlier *Neith-like* mother goddess named *Nammu*. Even now I actively seek out alternate sources of information on any topic that is of importance to me, in the fervent hope that each new author might include some tidbit of information that suddenly completes some unfinished puzzle for me.

When I first realized that I was pursuing a goal with my research, I thought that it was simply to define the attributes of what I saw as an "original" creation story–one that included the common elements of the Sumerian, Akkadian, Babylonian, Egyptian and Dogon traditions. I could see that there were enough common elements to suggest that these traditions had all evolved from a single source. I understood that the quest to identify these similarities might bring with it other new insights into the earliest creation traditions, but that possibility seemed like icing on the cake, not as any ultimate goal to be sought. The scattered symbols and stories which appeared to tie these ancient mythologies together were by no means complete enough to make any kind of overall sense.

Late in the 1990's I acquired a copy of *The Pale Fox*– the English translation of Marcel Griaule and Germaine Dieterlen's anthropological study of the Dogon. The detail it provided about Dogon religious symbols and mythology was frankly overwhelming. I could see that the Dogon stories were clearly speaking in metaphor, but with my limited experience with Dogon symbols the metaphors were in no way decipherable. What I did come away with after reading it was a clear professional sense that the symbols had been deliberately designed, but for me they were still just random symbols without a context. Studying them was like watching a foreign movie without subtitles–it was possible to get an overall sense of purpose and direction, but not much more. Years later I was to make contact with Dr. Stephen C. Infantino, the Humboldt State University professor who composed the English translation of *The Pale Fox*. He mentioned that he had suspected during the translation of the anthropological study that the Dogon creation story might represent more than mere tribal myths.

Based on a suggestion in Robert Temple's book, I purchased and began to study a copy of E.A. Wallis Budge's **Hieroglyphic Dictionary**, trying to develop a sense of how the hieroglyphic language was constructed. In some cases, the specific characters used to form a hieroglyphic word seemed to directly describe the word. For instance, an entry for the word *good* consists of a picture of a mother and a baby–very much like the Chinese pictogram for *good*. But in other cases there seemed to be no obvious relationship between the hieroglyphic characters and the concept conveyed by the word. I also began to read studies of other primitive mythologies, like the book **Alpha: The Myths of Creation**, which summarizes many different creation traditions.

In January of 2000 I stumbled upon a clue that was to prove to be the key that would unlock many doors for me in my understanding of Dogon symbolism. The pivotal event was both figuratively and literally a repetition of the story of Helen Keller's discovery of language. I was struggling with the most obvious theme of the Dogon creation story–the recurring references to *water*. I had just re-read Marcel Griaule's quote from Ogotemmeli about the nature of water and was perusing an encyclopedia article on water, trying to recount the most basic scientific facts and attributes of water. I happened across a series of sentences which seemed very familiar to me, even though I was reading them for the first time. It occurred to me that the words were familiar because they restated *almost verbatim* one of Marcel Griaule's quotes of Ogotemmeli. I compared the passages and verified that they indeed nearly matched. The parallel nature of the sentences seemed more than coincidental, and it made me wonder if the Dogon creation story was somehow a mask for what was essentially encyclopedic information about *water.* If so, then I had possibly discovered the missing element I most desperately needed—a possible context within which to interpret the Dogon symbols.

I began to review the events of the Dogon, Sumerian and Egyptian creation stories looking specifically for information about *water,* and what I found were metaphors for each of the significant scientific attributes of water—its molecular structure, its three physical states, and each of the stages of the natural water cycle. More importantly, I realized that if I used the encyclopedia article on water as a guide and simply followed its main points, it outlined for me the next corresponding element that I was to find in the Dogon creation story. This discovery changed the entire nature of my approach to understanding the episodes of Dogon mythology presented in **The Pale Fox**. Suddenly I was now devoting my effort to the task of understanding the *context* of each episode, hoping to find a much-needed shortcut for interpreting the meaning of each one.

My success in relating the encyclopedia article on water to the symbols and events of the Dogon creation story led me to pursue similarities between Dogon symbols and the sciences of human reproduction. I was astounded to discover that I could again follow the major topics of a related encyclopedia article and find similar themes within the Dogon creation story. I began to see the creation story itself as a kind of encyclopedia of information, and found myself turning again and again to modern encyclopedia articles to help interpret it.

What followed over the next year were almost daily insights into the meanings of the symbols that I had been studying for the prior five years. Each evening I would come home from work with a target list of words and concepts to explore in the hieroglyphic dictionary, testing the boundaries of correspondence between the Egyptian and Dogon creation traditions. My wife and I also subscribe to a thin weekly science magazine called **Science News**, which provides a brief summary of the week's events in science. As often as not when I read it, I learned some new fact from the cutting edge of science which conformed to or confirmed some aspect of Dogon mythology. My family and friends tolerated my growing preoccupation with the subject, and offered suggestions which sometimes proved to be quite helpful. My wife's insights into Judaism were of great help on many occasions, and my son and daughter often reported helpful details they learned in school about topics related to mine. One afternoon my daughter excitedly recognized a Dogon drawing as a representation of chromosomes and spindles based on diagrams she had seen in her high school biology class. My son made the connection between the Dogon numerological assignments of the numbers four and three as *male and female*, and the number of branches in the X and Y chromosomes.

At this point in my understanding, it struck me as rather far-fetched that an ancient creation story could be conveying information about subjects like the quantum structure of an atom. So for a period of time, I consciously discarded clues like pellets of clay and spiraling coils—possible metaphors for *particles and waves*—simply because I did not believe that a myth could be leading me in the direction of quantum theory. By February of 2000 I realized that I had acquired insights worth writing about, and that I was ready to compose what I expected would be a 20-page article, to record what I had learned. Because I was still actively learning about my subject as I wrote, the first draft took a journal-like form, recording each new revelation as I discovered it—some pertinent, and some not. After several weeks, the "article" had reached 40 pages, and I believed that I had exhausted all that I would ever have to say on the subject.

The Dogon images of particles and waves continued their nagging insistence, so I decided to re-read Stephen Hawking's **A Brief History of Time**. By this point my education in Dogon and Egyptian mythological symbols had come along far enough that I now recognized several of Hawkings' descriptions and diagrams as counterparts to familiar entries in **The Pale Fox**. I was able to identify the shape of Hawking's diagram of the event-horizon of a black hole as *Amma's egg*, and his description of the four categories of quantum particles as the Dogon drawing of the *germination of the sene*. These discoveries convinced me that, not only was I on the right track in my analysis of Dogon mythological symbols, but also that whatever source originally composed them knew more about the fundamentals of science than I did. From that point forward, I quietly assumed the role of student and the Dogon creation story became the teacher.

I was still left with important details, symbols and diagrams from **The Pale Fox** which I felt were related to the structure of matter, but which I still could not understand. Since the Dogon symbols had thus far led me to details of atomic and quantum structure, I decided to educate myself about the science of *string theory* and purchased **The Elegant Universe** by Brian Greene. One evening while reading it I stopped dead in my tracks at page 145 as I came to the diagram of vibrational patterns of quantum strings, because I realized that I was staring at the very image of one of the Dogon drawings that had eluded my understanding. After that I was not the least bit surprised that the remainder of Brian Greene's book confirmed item after item in Griaule and Dieterlen's book.

Once my correlations had been made between Dogon myth and science, the next step was to test my own initial theory—that the Dogon and Egyptian religions represent two versions of the same original tradition. If my interpretation of the Dogon symbols and their scientific meanings was correct, then I should find evidence of the same science in the major Egyptian creation traditions. I concluded that the best source for finding this evidence was the hieroglyphic dictionary.

As it turns out, the initial choice to compare Dogon and Egyptian symbols was a most fortuituous one, because the unchanged nature of the Egyptian hieroglyphs provided me with a reliable tool for establishing the underlying scientific meanings of Egyptian words. My intention had always been to become literate with Egyptian hieroglyphs. But at this point in my research, a lack of formal study of the language proved to be an asset, because it allowed me to infer likely meanings for various symbols without the prejudice of their established meanings. I should emphasize that in every case, I have presumed that the interpretive work that has been done by many respected scholars over many years on the Egyptian hieroglyphic language is correct. But one finds frequent references in ancient sources to a *secret language* of the Egyptian priests, and for me, the possibility of alternate meanings for any given hieroglyphic character or word falls well within the realm of believability. This is especially true when the new proposed meaning succeeds in reconnecting the characters of the hieroglyphic word to the concept that the word expresses.

In 2001 I read a mathematical analysis of Dogon symbols called **Ethnomathematics and Symbolic Thought: The Culture of the Dogon** by Teresa Vergani, a French mathematician, artist and poet from Portugal. I had been looking for someone with knowledge of Dogon symbols who might be interested in discussing my manuscript. The article clearly demonstrated the author's familiarity with and fondness for Dogon mythology, so I decided to contact her and ask if she would consider reviewing a draft of my text. She most generously agreed, then carefully read what I had written and offered her insights and suggestions. To my benefit, what started as only a distant professional contact has now turned into a most important and valuable friendship.

A major turning point in my study came in March and April of 2002, when I again focused my attention on the details of string theory. I purchased a copy of a book called

The Matter Myth by Paul Davies and John Gribbin which presented several diagrams relating to string theory. Of particular interest to me was a diagram which illustrated two types of simple quantum string intersections, whose shapes seemed somehow familiar. At about the same time I began to explore the hieroglyphic characters used in various forms of the Egyptian word "to weave", or *ntt*. The first two examples presented in Budge's hieroglyphic dictionary were spelled using figures which matched each of the diagrams of the two simple quantum string intersections. This discovery quickly led me to review the various spellings of the name of the Egyptian goddess *Neith*. I found that one form of the goddess' name was written using the diagram of the complex quantum string interaction.

There were still a series of diagrams from *The Pale Fox* that seemed to relate to the behavior of quantum strings, but whose significance had eluded me for several years. These diagrams show the seven evolutions of the vibrations within the *po*. My success at finding validation for string theory in the hieroglyphs spurred me to look again for scientific counterparts to the Dogon diagrams. This time what I found was a specific discussion of the 7-dimensional Cabali-Yau space from M-theory. As I had previously surmised, the details of how quantum strings vibrate within 7D space were in close agreement with the Dogon descriptions and diagrams.

I now realized that the string theory diagrams constituted proof of Egyptian science. The name of the Egyptian goddess who was responsible for the mythological creation of matter and the words for the method by which she created it were expressed in the clearest of terms of what could only be interpreted as string theory. No well-meaning critic could claim that an anthropologist had implanted it, nor was there much basis for suggesting that the resemblace was a coincidence, since the hieroglyphs reproduced not merely *one* but *three* separate scientific diagrams. And most important was the context in which the symbols were found–

as part of an explicit discussion of the creation of matter. This context had been firmly established by document after document from the beginning to the end of Egyptian culture. The astounding implications of these three ordinary hieroglyphic words were somewhat staggering. They meant that the resemblances between Dogon mythology and science were far more than wishful thinking. They also implied that the mythologies of the world could actually be telling the truth when they say that the skills of civilization were taught to humanity.

As a consequence, I now believe that the floodgates have opened—it is distinctly possible that there is new science to be found in the Egyptian hieroglyphs—those remarkable 5000 year-old drawings whose mysteries could well provide important clues to modern scientists. Moreover, the very existence of these astonishing symbols among the texts of ancient societies calls for an adjustment in the way that we understand and interpret our own history. These symbols also confront us with a host of new and difficult questions, many of which must eventually be answered. The foremost of these may be to ask (this time in all seriousness) who it was who took such great care to help us organize our earliest societies? Who was it who was so very concerned about our eventual development that they encoded these essential facts of science into the symbols and stories of our mythologies? We know that many of the most ancient sources considered these teachers to be gods—and surely a person from 3400 BC would have perceived them as gods. But the Dogon priests insist that they were not gods, and say that they referred to themselves simply as 'agents of god'. Whatever the case may be, there are a few simple observations that can be made about these teachers with some degree of certainty: They knew a *lot* about science—perhaps more than our scientists know today. Whoever they were, they demonstrated an absolute commitment to helping us. And in the end, they went to *very great lengths* to encode and preserve their message in ways that were carefully calculated to survive, and that were eventually meant to be discovered and recognized. I consider this book a call to the curious and the informed to keep looking for truthful answers to the difficult questions of the world, and as a challenge to those who are *more than able*, to continue to reach out generously to those who are *not yet able*.

References

Aveni, Anthony. *Stairways to the Stars*, John Wiley & Sons, Inc., New York, 1997

Baldwin, Neil. *Legends of the Plumed Serpent*, Public Affairs, New York, 1998

Barnstone, Willis. *The Other Bible*, Harper San Francisco, San Francisco, 1984. By permission.

Basan, Markus and Basan, Claus *String Theory and M-Theory*, on-line article.

Bauval, Robert and Gilbert, Adrian. *The Orion Mystery*, Crown Publishers, Inc., New York, 1994

Best, Elsdon. *Maori Religion and Mythology*, W.A.G Skinner, Government Printer, Wellington, New Zealand, 1924

Black, Jeremy and Green, Anthony. *Gods, Demons and Symbols of Ancient Mesopotamia,* University of Texas Press, Austin,1997

Budge, E.A. Wallis, *An Egyptian Hieroglyphic Dictionary,* Dover, New York, 1978

Budge, E.A. Wallis, *Egyptian Language–Lessons in Egyptian Hieroglyphics*, Dorset Press, New York, 1993

Budge, E.A. Wallis, *Legends of the Egyptian Gods*, Dover, New York, 1994

Budge, E.A. Wallis, *The Gods of the Egyptians*, Dover, New York, 1994

Bulfinch, Thomas, *Age of Fable*, Dell Publishing Co., New York, 1959

Calame-Griaule, Genevieve. *Dictionnaire Dogon*, Librarie C. Klincksieck, Paris

Caubet, Annie and Pouyssegur, Patrick. *The Ancient Near*

East, Terrail, Paris 1997; English edition, Bayard Presse SA, 1998

Clark, R.T. Rundle. *Myth and Symbol in Ancient Egypt,* Thames and Hudson, London, 1995

Clarke, Hyde. *Serpent and Siva Worship and Mythology in Central America, Africa and Asia,* J.W. Bouten, New York 1877.

Cotterell, Arthur and Storm, Rachel. *The Ultimate Encyclopedia of Mythology,* Lorenz Books, 1999, permission requested.

Davies, Paul and Gribben, John *The Matter Myth,* Simon & Schuster/Touchstone, New York, 1992, permission requested.

Dozier, Jr., Rush W. *Codes of Evolution,* Crown Publishers, Inc., New York, 1992. By permission.

Duncan, David Ewing. *Calendar,* Avon Books, Inc., New York, 1998

Encarta 97 Encyclopedia, Microsoft, 1993-1996

Feynman, Richard P. *The Character of Physical Law,* The MIT Press, Boston, 1967. By permission

Forde, Daryll *African Worlds,* Oxford University Press, London, 1954; reprinted 1999 by James Currey Publishers and LIT Verlag for the International African Institute, with a new introduction by Wendy James.

Gill, Joseph B. *The Great Pyramid Speaks,* Barnes & Noble Books, New York, 1984. By permission.

Graves, Robert *New Larousse Encyclopedia of Mythology,* Hamlyn Publishing Group Limited, London, 1968

Greene, Brian *The Elegant Universe,* Vintage Books, 2000, permission requested.

Griaule, Marcel and Dieterlen, Germaine. *The Dogon,* an essay from *African Worlds: Studies in the Cosmological Ideas and Social Values of African Peoples,* Oxford University Press, London, 1954

Griaule, Marcel. *Conversations with Ogotemmeli,* Oxford University Press, 1970, permission requested.

Griaule, Marcel and Dieterlen, Germaine. *A Sudanese Sirius System*, 1950, reprinted by permission in *The Sirius Mystery* by Robert K.G. Temple

Griaule, Marcel and Dieterlen, Germaine. *The Pale Fox*, Continuum Foundation, 1986 Originally published in French as *Le renard pale* by l'Intitut d'Ethnologie, Paris, 1965, by permission of Afrikan World Books, PO Box 16447, Baltimore, MD 21217.

Grimal, Nicholas. *A History of Ancient Egypt*, Blackwell, Oxford UK and Cambridge USA, 1994

Griffis-Greenberg, Katherine *Neith: Goddess of the Beginning, the Beyond, and the End* On-line article at www.geocities.com/Athens/Acropolis/ 8669/neith.html, 1999, permission requested.

Hamilton, Edith. *Mythology: Timeless Tales of Gods and Heroes*, Warner Books, New York, 1999. By permission.

Hancock, Graham. *Fingerprints of the Gods,* Crown Publishers, Inc., New York, 1995

Hancock, Graham, and Bauval, Robert. *The Message of the Sphinx*, Crown Publishers, Inc., New York, 1996

Hapgood, Charles. *Maps of the Ancient Sea Kings*, Adventures Unlimited Press, Kempton, IL, 1966

Hart, George. *A Dictionary of Egyptian Gods and Goddesses*, Routledge, London and New York, 1999, permission requested.

Hawking, Stephen W. *A Brief History of Time*, Bantam Books, Toronto, 1988. By permission.

Higgins, Godfrey *Anacalypsis*, Kessinger Publishing Company, Montana, U.S.A., permission requested.

Jacq, Christian. *Fascinating Hieroglyphs*, Sterling Publishing Co, Inc., New York, 1996. By permission.

Krauss, Lawrence M. *Atom: An Odyssey from the Big Bang to Life on Earth . . . and Beyond*, Little, Brown and Company, Boston, New York, London, 2001

Long, Charles H. *Alpha: The Myths of Creation*, George Braziller, New York, 1963, permission requested.

Mercantante, Anthony S. *Facts on File Encyclopedia of World Mythology and Legend,* Facts On File, New York and Oxford, 1988

Merriam-Webster's Encyclopedia of World Religions, Merriam-Webster, Springfield, MA, 1999

Miller, Mary and Taube, Karl *The Gods and Symbols of Ancient Mexico and the Maya,* Thames and Hudson, London, 1993. By permission.

Moore, George Foot, *Judaism in the First Centuries of the Christian Era: Volume 1–The Age of Tannaim,* Schocken Books, New York, 1971. By permission.

Newsweek Magazine, May 8, 2000, Newsweek, Inc., New York, 2000

Ouaknin, Marc-Alain *Symbols of Judaism,* Assouline Publishing, New York, 2000, permission requested.

Pritchard, James B. *Ancient Near Eastern Texts, Third Edition,* Princeton University Press, Princeton, NJ, 1969

Quirke, Stephen *Ancient Egyptian Religion,* British Museum Press, London, 1992

Rice, Michael *Egypt's Making: The Origins of Ancient Egypt, 5000-2000 BC,* Routledge, London, 1991, permission requested.

Saggs, H.W.F. *Civilization Before Greece and Rome,* Yale University Press, New Haven and London, 1989

Sauneron, Serge *The Priests of Ancient Egypt,* Cornell University Press, Ithaca and London, 2000. By permission.

Science News, Vol 156, No. 18. Science Service, Marion, OH, 1999

Science News, Vol 157, No. 13. Science Service, Marion, OH, 2000

Science News, *Vol 158, No. 5.* Science Service, Marion, OH, 2000

Science News, *Vol 158, No. 9.* Science Service, Marion, OH, 2000

Seleem, R. Ramses, *The Illustrated Egyptian Book of the*

Dead, Sterling Publishing Company, Inc., New York, 2001. By permission.

Temple, Robert K.G. *The Sirius Mystery*, Destiny Books, Rochester, Vermont, 1987, permission requested.

Tomkins, Peter. *Secrets of the Great Pyramid*, Galahad Books, New York, 1971, permission requested.

Trepp, Leo. *The Complete Book of Jewish Observance*, Summit Books, New York, 1980, 1981 (C) copyright Behrman House, Inc., www.behrmanhouse.com. By permission.

Velikovsky, Immanuel. *Ages in Chaos*, Doubleday & Company, Inc., Garden City, NY, 1952

Velikovsky, Immanuel. *Oedipus and Akhnaton*, Doubleday & Company, Inc., Garden City, NY, 1960

Velikovsky, Immanuel. *Worlds in Collision*, The MacMillan Company, New York, 1950

Vergani, Teresa. *Ethnomathematics and Symbolic Thought: The Culture of the Dogon* On-line article, 1999

Wake, C. Staniland. *The Origin of Serpent Worship*, J.W.Bouten, New York, 1877

Webster's Seventh New Collegiate Dictionary, G. & C. Merriam Company, Springfield, MA, 1967

Wigoder, Geoffrey, *Encyclopedic Dictionary of Judaica*, Leon Amiel Publisher, New York, 1974, permission requested.

World Book 2002 Standard Edition, Microsoft, 2002

Printed in the United States
1457100002B/136-138